Machine Identity Management: Protecting Non-Human Identities in the Enterprise

James Relington

DEDICATION

To those who seek knowledge, inspiration, and new perspectives—
may this book be a companion on your journey, a spark for curiosity,
and a reminder that every page turned is a step toward discovery.

AKNOWLEDGEMENTS

I would like to express my deepest gratitude to everyone who contributed to the creation of this book. To my colleagues and mentors, your insights and expertise have been invaluable. A special thank you to my family and friends for their unwavering support and encouragement throughout this journey.

Introduction to Machine Identity Management

Machine identity management has become a critical component of modern cybersecurity strategies as enterprises increasingly rely on automated systems, cloud services, and interconnected devices. While traditional identity management focuses on human users, machine identities represent the authentication and authorization of non-human entities such as servers, applications, containers, IoT devices, and APIs. These identities enable secure communication, data exchange, and access to critical resources across complex IT environments. As enterprises scale their digital operations, managing machine identities becomes both a necessity and a challenge, requiring dedicated strategies, governance frameworks, and security measures.

The rapid evolution of technology has led to an explosion of machine identities across enterprise networks. Unlike human identities, which are relatively static and managed through user directories, machine identities are dynamic, constantly created and revoked as applications and services interact. Cloud computing, DevOps automation, and microservices architectures contribute to this increase by generating thousands or even millions of machine identities that must be managed efficiently. Without proper governance, enterprises risk identity sprawl, where unmanaged or orphaned machine identities become potential attack vectors for cybercriminals. Threat actors can exploit compromised machine identities to gain unauthorized access, deploy malware, or move laterally within networks undetected.

At the core of machine identity management is the concept of cryptographic credentials, primarily in the form of digital certificates and cryptographic keys. These credentials allow machines to authenticate securely, ensuring that communication between systems remains encrypted and protected from tampering. Public Key Infrastructure (PKI) plays a crucial role in issuing and managing digital certificates, providing trust across distributed networks. However, relying solely on traditional PKI mechanisms is no longer sufficient in modern, highly automated IT environments. Organizations must adopt scalable, automated solutions that integrate machine identity lifecycle management, ensuring that certificates are issued, rotated, and revoked without manual intervention.

The security risks associated with poor machine identity management are substantial. Expired certificates can lead to service disruptions, breaking critical business applications and causing costly downtime. Misconfigured certificates can expose sensitive data by allowing unauthorized parties to intercept encrypted communications. Cybercriminals increasingly target machine identities to impersonate legitimate systems, bypass security controls, and establish persistent access within an organization's infrastructure. The consequences of machine identity compromise range from data breaches and financial loss to reputational damage and regulatory non-compliance. To mitigate these risks, enterprises must enforce strict policies governing the issuance, renewal, and expiration of machine identities while implementing robust monitoring and detection capabilities to identify suspicious activity.

Automation is essential to managing machine identities effectively. Given the volume and complexity of machine identities in modern enterprises, manual management processes are impractical and prone to human error. Organizations must leverage identity orchestration tools, automated certificate management platforms, and policy-based frameworks to maintain control over machine identities. Automated solutions enable real-time visibility into certificate usage, detect anomalies, and enforce compliance with security standards. Integrating machine identity management with existing identity and access management (IAM) systems further enhances security by ensuring that machine identities follow the same governance principles as human identities.

The shift to cloud computing and multi-cloud environments has introduced additional challenges to machine identity management. Each cloud provider has its own mechanisms for handling machine identities, requiring organizations to establish a unified approach that works across multiple platforms. Containers and Kubernetes clusters generate short-lived machine identities that require continuous monitoring and rotation. Secure API communication, which relies on authentication mechanisms such as OAuth and mutual TLS, also demands robust machine identity management to prevent unauthorized access. Without a cohesive strategy, organizations risk losing visibility and control over their machine identities, exposing themselves to security gaps and compliance violations.

Regulatory frameworks and industry standards emphasize the importance of securing machine identities. Compliance requirements such as GDPR, HIPAA, PCI-DSS, and NIST guidelines mandate the protection of sensitive data and secure authentication practices, which extend to machine identities. Organizations that fail to implement proper machine identity management strategies risk non-compliance penalties and potential legal liabilities. Auditing and reporting capabilities are essential for demonstrating compliance, requiring enterprises to maintain logs of certificate issuance, usage, and revocation. A well-defined governance model ensures that machine identities align with organizational security policies and regulatory mandates.

Despite the challenges, organizations that invest in robust machine identity management gain significant security and operational benefits. By ensuring that every machine identity is authenticated, encrypted, and properly managed, enterprises can reduce the risk of unauthorized access, prevent data breaches, and maintain seamless business operations. A proactive approach to machine identity security enhances trust within the organization and strengthens defenses against emerging cyber threats. As the digital landscape continues to evolve, machine identity management will remain a fundamental pillar of enterprise security, requiring continuous innovation and adaptation to meet the demands of modern IT environments.

The Rise of Non-Human Identities in the Enterprise

Enterprises today are undergoing a profound shift in how identities are managed, as the number of non-human identities surpasses human users across corporate networks. These non-human identities include applications, workloads, cloud services, IoT devices, robotic process automation (RPA) bots, APIs, and various other digital entities that require authentication and authorization. Unlike human identities, which are relatively static and managed through user directories and role-based access control, non-human identities are dynamic, ephemeral, and exponentially growing. Organizations must now address the challenges associated with securing these identities to prevent unauthorized access, data breaches, and operational disruptions.

The proliferation of cloud computing, DevOps automation, and microservices architectures has accelerated the adoption of non-human identities in enterprises. Cloud providers generate machine identities for virtual machines, storage accounts, and databases. Containers and serverless functions create short-lived identities that enable them to communicate securely. DevOps pipelines rely on secrets, API keys, and certificates to automate deployments and integrations. Each of these elements requires proper identity management to ensure secure interactions between systems, but the scale and complexity of managing them manually have become infeasible. Without effective governance, non-human identities can become untracked, leading to security blind spots and increasing the risk of credential theft.

Non-human identities are now critical to business operations, enabling everything from AI-driven decision-making to automated security responses. In financial institutions, algorithms process transactions and communicate with external payment systems, requiring digital certificates and authentication mechanisms. In healthcare, medical devices connect to hospital networks, transmitting patient data through encrypted channels. In industrial settings, smart sensors and connected machinery operate autonomously, interacting with cloud-based analytics platforms. The reliance on non-human identities extends beyond IT infrastructure into every aspect of the business, making their protection a top security priority.

Cybercriminals recognize the growing importance of non-human identities and actively exploit them to infiltrate enterprise networks. Compromised API keys allow attackers to access sensitive data and disrupt critical services. Stolen certificates enable adversaries to impersonate trusted applications, bypassing security controls and executing malicious operations. Misconfigured service accounts with excessive privileges can become entry points for lateral movement within a network, leading to ransomware attacks or data exfiltration. Unlike human accounts, which often have multi-factor authentication (MFA) and strict monitoring, machine identities frequently lack robust security measures, making them attractive targets for cyber threats.

The sheer volume of non-human identities in an enterprise environment presents a governance challenge. Each application, system, and automated process may require multiple credentials, leading to identity sprawl if not properly managed. Orphaned credentials—those left behind when applications are decommissioned or systems change—pose a significant risk, as attackers can exploit them for unauthorized access. Expired certificates, when not renewed in time, can cause critical service outages, disrupting business continuity. Organizations must establish comprehensive policies to track, audit, and manage the entire lifecycle of non-human identities, ensuring that they are issued securely, rotated regularly, and revoked when no longer needed.

Regulatory and compliance requirements increasingly emphasize the need for securing non-human identities. Standards such as NIST, ISO 27001, PCI-DSS, and GDPR mandate proper authentication, encryption, and access controls for all identities, including non-human ones. Enterprises must demonstrate compliance by maintaining audit logs, enforcing strict access policies, and implementing automated identity management solutions. Failure to comply with these regulations can result in financial penalties, legal consequences, and reputational damage. Security teams must ensure that non-human identities adhere to the same rigorous security standards as human identities to meet regulatory expectations and minimize risk exposure.

To address the challenges posed by non-human identities, enterprises are investing in automation and orchestration solutions that integrate with existing identity and access management (IAM) frameworks. Automated certificate management platforms streamline the issuance, renewal, and revocation of digital certificates, reducing the likelihood of expired or misconfigured credentials. Secrets management solutions securely store API keys, passwords, and cryptographic keys, preventing unauthorized access. Policy-based access control mechanisms enforce least privilege principles, ensuring that non-human identities only have the permissions necessary to perform their functions. By implementing these technologies, organizations gain greater visibility and control over their expanding identity ecosystem.

The role of artificial intelligence and machine learning in managing non-human identities is also gaining traction. AI-driven security solutions analyze identity behaviors, detecting anomalies that may indicate a compromised machine identity. These systems can identify unusual patterns, such as an API key being used from an unexpected location or a certificate being leveraged outside of its intended environment. By leveraging AI for continuous monitoring, enterprises can respond to threats in real time, mitigating the impact of identity-related breaches. The combination of automation and intelligence is essential in addressing the growing scale and complexity of non-human identity management.

As organizations embrace digital transformation, the rise of non-human identities will continue to accelerate. Enterprises must adopt a proactive approach to identity security, implementing governance frameworks, security policies, and automation tools that address the unique challenges posed by non-human entities. The ability to secure and manage these identities effectively will determine the resilience of an organization's security posture in an era where machines outnumber human users in the enterprise environment. By recognizing the importance of non-human identities and taking strategic measures to protect them, enterprises can safeguard their critical assets, maintain compliance, and reduce the risk of cyber threats.

Why Machine Identities Matter

Machine identities have become an essential aspect of enterprise security, enabling secure communication between applications, services, devices, and cloud environments. As organizations continue to adopt cloud computing, automation, and interconnected technologies, machine identities play a critical role in establishing trust and protecting sensitive data. Unlike human identities, which rely on usernames, passwords, and multi-factor authentication, machine identities use cryptographic credentials such as digital certificates, API keys, and SSH keys to authenticate and authorize interactions. Without proper management, these identities become a significant security risk, providing an entry point for cybercriminals to exploit vulnerabilities, impersonate trusted entities, and gain unauthorized access to critical systems.

The sheer volume of machine identities in modern enterprises is staggering. Every cloud workload, container, microservice, IoT device, and software-defined infrastructure component requires its own unique identity to function securely. These identities ensure that machines can authenticate with each other without human intervention, enabling automated processes to run smoothly.

However, with the exponential growth of non-human entities, organizations struggle to maintain visibility and control over their machine identities. Poorly managed identities lead to security gaps, making it easier for attackers to compromise credentials and exploit them for malicious purposes. Machine identity sprawl has become a growing concern, with many enterprises unaware of the full scope of their identity landscape.

Cybercriminals have recognized the value of machine identities and are increasingly targeting them to bypass security controls. Unlike user credentials, which often have additional security layers such as multi-factor authentication and strict access policies, machine identities are frequently left unprotected. Attackers who gain access to compromised certificates, API keys, or encryption keys can move laterally within a network, posing as legitimate applications or services. This type of attack is difficult to detect because the malicious activity appears to originate from a trusted source. Stolen machine identities enable threat actors to manipulate data, intercept communications, and execute unauthorized transactions without triggering traditional security alarms.

Mismanagement of machine identities can lead to severe operational disruptions. Expired digital certificates are a common cause of service outages, breaking critical applications, websites, and APIs. When certificates are not renewed in time, encrypted connections fail, leading to downtime that impacts business operations and customer trust. In industries such as finance, healthcare, and government, these disruptions can have legal and regulatory consequences. Organizations that lack automated certificate management solutions often face difficulties keeping track of expiration dates, increasing the likelihood of unexpected failures. Ensuring that machine identities are continuously monitored and renewed is essential for maintaining seamless business operations.

The security implications of weak machine identity management extend beyond service disruptions. Organizations that fail to protect their machine identities risk data breaches, intellectual property theft, and compliance violations. Many compliance frameworks, including GDPR, HIPAA, PCI-DSS, and NIST guidelines, mandate the use of strong authentication and encryption for protecting sensitive data.

Machine identities are a fundamental component of these security controls, ensuring that only authorized systems can access or transmit data. A failure to enforce strict identity policies can result in non-compliance penalties, reputational damage, and legal repercussions. Security teams must implement governance frameworks that enforce identity best practices across the entire enterprise.

One of the biggest challenges in managing machine identities is the need for automation. Unlike human identities, which remain relatively stable over time, machine identities are constantly created, used, rotated, and retired. In cloud environments, virtual machines and containers may only exist for a few minutes before being replaced by new instances. Traditional manual processes for managing credentials are no longer viable, as they introduce inefficiencies, human errors, and security gaps. Enterprises must adopt automated solutions that provide visibility, enforce policies, and seamlessly integrate with existing security frameworks. Identity orchestration tools and certificate management platforms help organizations scale their identity management efforts without compromising security.

The concept of zero trust security has further highlighted the importance of machine identities. In a zero trust architecture, no entity—human or machine—is automatically trusted, and every interaction must be authenticated and verified. Machine identities ensure that applications, APIs, and workloads can securely communicate in a zero trust environment. Without strong identity management, organizations cannot enforce the core principles of zero trust, leaving their networks vulnerable to lateral movement and privilege escalation attacks. Implementing machine identity security as part of a broader zero trust strategy is essential for modern cybersecurity resilience.

As the digital landscape continues to evolve, the role of machine identities in enterprise security will only become more critical. The ongoing expansion of cloud computing, AI-driven automation, and interconnected devices will further increase the number of machine identities that organizations must manage. Enterprises that fail to address machine identity security risk falling behind in their security posture, exposing themselves to emerging threats and compliance challenges. By prioritizing machine identity protection, organizations can build a more secure, resilient, and trustworthy digital ecosystem that supports innovation and operational efficiency.

Understanding the Threat Landscape for Machine Identities

The rapid expansion of machine identities in enterprise environments has introduced a new and complex threat landscape that organizations must address. As the number of non-human entities continues to grow, cybercriminals have shifted their focus from targeting traditional user accounts to exploiting machine identities. These identities, which include digital certificates, API keys, SSH keys, and service accounts, are often left unprotected, making them an attractive target for attackers seeking to bypass security controls and gain unauthorized access to critical systems. The lack of visibility, improper lifecycle management, and weak security policies surrounding machine identities have created significant vulnerabilities that adversaries can exploit for financial gain, data breaches, and persistent network infiltration.

One of the primary threats to machine identities is credential theft and misuse. Unlike human credentials, which typically require multi-factor authentication and are actively monitored for suspicious activity, machine identities are often overlooked in security strategies. Cybercriminals use various techniques to steal API keys, digital certificates, and cryptographic secrets, allowing them to impersonate legitimate applications or services. Once attackers gain access to a compromised machine identity, they can establish persistence within a network, move laterally, and escalate privileges without triggering traditional security alerts. The stolen credentials can also be sold on the dark web, providing other malicious actors with access to enterprise systems.

Man-in-the-middle attacks present another major risk to machine identities, particularly in environments where communication between applications and services relies on encrypted connections. If an attacker is able to intercept or manipulate digital certificates, they can impersonate trusted entities and decrypt sensitive data in transit. This type of attack is especially dangerous in cloud environments, where organizations rely on machine identities for authentication and data exchange between microservices. Weak or misconfigured certificate management practices increase the risk of man-in-the-middle attacks, as expired or improperly issued certificates can be exploited to establish fraudulent trust relationships.

Expired machine identities represent a hidden yet critical security risk for enterprises. Many organizations fail to track the lifecycle of their digital certificates, leading to unexpected expiration that can cause service disruptions or security gaps. Attackers often take advantage of expired certificates by registering similar domain names and issuing fraudulent certificates to impersonate legitimate services. This form of identity spoofing allows cybercriminals to conduct phishing attacks, deploy malware, and exfiltrate sensitive data under the guise of a trusted entity. Organizations that lack automated certificate renewal and monitoring mechanisms are especially vulnerable to these tactics, as manually tracking thousands of machine identities is impractical.

Supply chain attacks have also become a significant threat to machine identities, particularly in environments where enterprises rely on third-party vendors and cloud providers. Attackers target software supply chains by injecting malicious code into dependencies, exploiting insecure API integrations, and leveraging compromised service accounts to infiltrate enterprise networks. Machine identities play a crucial role in securing these supply chain interactions, but when improperly managed, they can become the weakest link in an organization's security posture. A single compromised machine identity in the supply chain can grant attackers access to multiple interconnected systems, allowing them to move undetected across various environments.

The rise of ransomware and advanced persistent threats (APTs) has further exposed the vulnerabilities associated with machine identities. Modern ransomware groups are increasingly leveraging machine identities to execute automated attacks at scale. By exploiting weakly secured service accounts and API keys, ransomware operators can encrypt critical enterprise data, disable security controls, and exfiltrate sensitive information before demanding a ransom. APT groups, on the other hand, use machine identities to establish long-term access within enterprise networks, often remaining undetected for months or even years. These adversaries carefully study identity management weaknesses, using stolen credentials to bypass security measures and maintain persistence without raising suspicion.

Shadow IT and identity sprawl contribute to the growing threat landscape by creating unmanaged and unmonitored machine identities. In many organizations, developers, engineers, and business units create machine identities outside of official security policies, leading to an uncontrolled expansion of identities across cloud and on-premises environments. These identities often lack proper governance, making them an easy target for attackers seeking to exploit untracked credentials. Security teams struggle to identify and secure these unmanaged identities, increasing the risk of unauthorized access, data exposure, and compliance violations. Without comprehensive visibility into machine identity usage, organizations cannot effectively protect their digital assets.

The increasing sophistication of cyber threats has made it clear that machine identities must be treated with the same level of security as human identities. Attackers are continuously developing new methods to exploit identity weaknesses, from credential stuffing and certificate abuse to API hijacking and malware injections. Organizations that fail to implement strong identity governance frameworks, automate certificate management, and enforce least privilege access controls will remain vulnerable to machine identity-related breaches. The need for continuous monitoring, proactive threat detection, and secure identity lifecycle management has never been greater as enterprises navigate an evolving cyber threat landscape.

Key Components of Machine Identity Management

Machine identity management is an essential aspect of enterprise security, ensuring that non-human entities such as applications, services, cloud workloads, IoT devices, and APIs are properly authenticated and authorized to communicate securely. As organizations continue to scale their digital operations, managing machine identities has become increasingly complex, requiring a structured approach that includes visibility, governance, automation, and security controls. Without a well-defined strategy, enterprises risk identity sprawl, unauthorized access, and potential breaches that can lead to severe financial and reputational consequences. A robust machine identity management framework consists of several key components that work together to establish a secure and efficient identity ecosystem.

One of the foundational components of machine identity management is authentication. Machine authentication enables systems, applications, and services to verify each other's identity before exchanging data or executing tasks. Unlike human authentication, which relies on usernames and passwords, machine authentication depends on cryptographic credentials such as digital certificates, API keys, SSH keys, and symmetric or asymmetric encryption keys. These credentials act as digital passports, ensuring that only authorized machines can interact within an enterprise environment. A strong authentication framework ensures that these credentials are securely generated, distributed, and validated throughout their lifecycle, preventing unauthorized entities from gaining access to sensitive systems.

Authorization is another critical component that defines the permissions and access levels assigned to machine identities. Once a machine has been authenticated, it must be granted the appropriate level of access based on predefined security policies. This process ensures that machines only perform the functions they are intended to, reducing the risk of privilege escalation and lateral movement within a network. Organizations must implement role-based access control (RBAC) and attribute-based access control (ABAC) frameworks to govern machine identities, ensuring that each entity operates within the least privilege model. By restricting access to only necessary resources, enterprises can mitigate the risk of identity compromise and unauthorized data exposure.

Identity lifecycle management is essential to maintaining a secure and organized machine identity ecosystem. The lifecycle of a machine identity includes creation, deployment, rotation, expiration, renewal, and decommissioning. Each phase of this lifecycle requires strict governance to prevent identity sprawl and security lapses. Without proper management, expired certificates, orphaned credentials, and unmonitored machine accounts can create vulnerabilities that attackers may exploit. Automating identity lifecycle processes helps organizations track and control machine identities efficiently, ensuring that credentials are regularly rotated, expired identities are removed, and policies are consistently enforced.

Certificate and key management play a crucial role in securing machine identities by protecting the cryptographic assets that enable secure communication. Digital certificates, issued by certificate authorities (CAs), validate the authenticity of machines in encrypted transactions. Organizations must implement a centralized certificate management system to oversee the issuance, renewal, and revocation of certificates across their IT infrastructure. Similarly, encryption keys used in APIs, secure shell (SSH) connections, and other cryptographic operations must be stored securely in hardware security modules (HSMs) or secrets management solutions. The improper handling of certificates and keys can lead to security breaches, service disruptions, and compliance violations, making effective management a necessity.

Visibility and monitoring are key components of machine identity management, allowing enterprises to detect unauthorized activity and prevent potential security threats. Continuous monitoring of machine identities provides insights into how credentials are being used, whether any anomalies are present, and if security policies are being followed. Organizations must leverage identity intelligence solutions that analyze machine identity behavior in real time, alerting security teams to potential risks such as unauthorized certificate usage, expired credentials, or abnormal access patterns. By maintaining visibility across all machine identities, enterprises can proactively address security concerns before they escalate into significant incidents.

Governance and compliance frameworks ensure that machine identity management aligns with industry regulations and internal security policies. Enterprises operating in highly regulated sectors such as finance, healthcare, and government must adhere to standards such as GDPR, HIPAA, PCI-DSS, and NIST guidelines, which mandate strict authentication and encryption practices. Implementing machine identity governance helps organizations enforce security controls, conduct regular audits, and generate compliance reports that demonstrate adherence to regulatory requirements. Strong governance reduces the risk of identity-related breaches and minimizes the potential for financial penalties resulting from non-compliance.

Automation is a fundamental component of modern machine identity management, reducing the operational burden associated with managing thousands or even millions of identities. Manual processes are not scalable and introduce human errors that can lead to security vulnerabilities. Enterprises must implement automated solutions for certificate issuance, renewal, and revocation, as well as secrets management tools that secure API keys and cryptographic credentials. Automated policy enforcement ensures that identity security best practices are consistently applied across the organization, eliminating gaps that could be exploited by attackers. Integrating automation with security information and event management (SIEM) platforms further enhances detection and response capabilities, ensuring that machine identity risks are addressed in real time.

Machine identity management also benefits from integration with identity and access management (IAM) platforms, unifying human and non-human identity security under a single framework. By consolidating machine identity governance with existing IAM policies, enterprises can streamline access controls, enforce consistent authentication mechanisms, and simplify compliance reporting. This integration enhances the overall security posture by ensuring that all identities, whether human or machine, are subject to the same rigorous security policies and oversight.

As enterprises continue to adopt cloud computing, DevOps automation, and microservices architectures, the importance of machine identity management will only grow. The security of modern digital ecosystems depends on the ability to authenticate and authorize machines with the same level of scrutiny as human users. A well-structured machine identity management framework provides the necessary controls to secure these identities, minimize risk, and ensure that business operations remain uninterrupted. Organizations that invest in robust authentication, authorization, lifecycle management, certificate governance, monitoring, compliance, and automation will be better equipped to protect their critical assets in an increasingly interconnected world.

Cryptographic Foundations of Machine Identities

Machine identities rely on cryptographic principles to ensure secure authentication, authorization, and communication between non-human entities such as applications, cloud workloads, APIs, and IoT devices. Unlike human identities, which use passwords and multi-factor authentication, machine identities depend on digital certificates, cryptographic keys, and encryption algorithms to establish trust in enterprise environments. The robustness of these cryptographic foundations determines the overall security of machine identity management, making it essential for organizations to implement strong encryption standards, key management practices, and secure cryptographic protocols to prevent unauthorized access, identity spoofing, and data breaches.

Public Key Infrastructure (PKI) serves as the backbone of machine identity security, enabling secure authentication through digital certificates. PKI operates on the principles of asymmetric cryptography, which involves a pair of cryptographic keys: a public key and a private key. The public key is used to encrypt data, while the private key is used to decrypt it, ensuring that only the intended recipient can access the transmitted information. In machine identity management, digital certificates issued by a trusted certificate authority (CA) bind public keys to specific machine identities, verifying their authenticity. These certificates enable secure connections between machines, preventing attackers from intercepting or tampering with sensitive data.

Symmetric cryptography plays a complementary role in securing machine identities by enabling fast and efficient encryption of data during machine-to-machine communication. Unlike asymmetric encryption, which relies on key pairs, symmetric encryption uses a single secret key for both encryption and decryption. This method is commonly employed in securing network protocols, encrypting API keys, and protecting sensitive credentials within enterprise systems. However, symmetric encryption requires secure key distribution mechanisms to prevent unauthorized access, as the exposure of a single key can compromise the confidentiality of encrypted communications. Organizations implement key management solutions and hardware security modules (HSMs) to store and distribute symmetric keys securely.

Secure hashing algorithms are another fundamental cryptographic component of machine identity security, ensuring the integrity of machine-generated data. Hashing functions convert input data into a fixed-length hash value, which acts as a unique digital fingerprint. In machine identity management, hashing is used to verify the integrity of certificates, authentication tokens, and cryptographic signatures. Hashing algorithms such as SHA-256 provide collision resistance, ensuring that no two different inputs generate the same hash value. Cryptographic hashing is crucial in detecting unauthorized modifications to machine identities and preventing tampering in certificate chains and API authentication mechanisms.

Digital signatures enhance the security of machine identities by providing proof of authenticity and non-repudiation. When a machine sends a request or transmits data, it signs the information using its private key. The recipient verifies the signature using the corresponding public key, ensuring that the message originates from a legitimate machine and has not been altered. Digital signatures are widely used in code signing, ensuring that software updates and applications come from trusted sources. In certificate-based authentication, signatures validate the trustworthiness of machine identities, preventing attackers from using counterfeit credentials to gain access to enterprise systems.

Secure key management is a critical aspect of maintaining the cryptographic foundations of machine identities. Organizations must implement strict policies for generating, storing, rotating, and revoking cryptographic keys to prevent unauthorized access and key misuse. Private keys should never be exposed or stored in plaintext, as their compromise can lead to identity spoofing and system breaches. Best practices include using hardware security modules (HSMs) to generate and store private keys in a tamper-resistant environment, implementing automated key rotation policies, and enforcing access controls to restrict key usage. Without proper key management, even the strongest encryption algorithms become ineffective, leaving machine identities vulnerable to attacks.

Certificate lifecycle management ensures the continuous security and validity of machine identities by automating the issuance, renewal, and revocation of digital certificates. Expired certificates can disrupt critical business operations, causing service outages and breaking secure connections. Attackers often exploit expired or misconfigured certificates to impersonate legitimate machines, conduct phishing attacks, and intercept encrypted communications. Organizations must deploy certificate management solutions that provide real-time monitoring, automated renewal, and alerts for expiring certificates. By maintaining an organized and up-to-date certificate inventory, enterprises reduce the risk of operational disruptions and security breaches.

The use of cryptographic protocols such as Transport Layer Security (TLS) strengthens the security of machine-to-machine communication. TLS encrypts data transmitted between systems, preventing eavesdropping, man-in-the-middle attacks, and data interception. Machine identities use TLS certificates to establish secure connections between web servers, APIs, and cloud services. Ensuring the correct implementation of TLS, including enforcing strong cipher suites, disabling outdated protocols, and regularly rotating certificates, enhances the resilience of machine identities against cyber threats. Organizations that fail to maintain proper TLS configurations risk exposing sensitive data to attackers who exploit weak encryption settings.

Quantum computing presents an emerging challenge to the cryptographic foundations of machine identities. As quantum computers advance, traditional encryption methods, particularly RSA and ECC-based cryptographic schemes, face the risk of being broken by quantum algorithms capable of factorizing large numbers exponentially faster than classical computers. To future-proof machine identity security, organizations must explore quantum-resistant cryptographic algorithms, such as lattice-based and hash-based encryption methods. Post-quantum cryptography initiatives aim to develop encryption standards that can withstand the computational power of quantum attacks, ensuring the long-term security of machine identities in enterprise environments.

Cryptographic access controls further reinforce machine identity security by restricting access to sensitive credentials and enforcing identity-based authentication. Role-based access control (RBAC) and attribute-based access control (ABAC) models ensure that only authorized machines and services can use cryptographic keys and certificates. Multi-factor authentication (MFA) for machines, which incorporates cryptographic tokens and identity assertions, adds an additional layer of security to protect machine identities from unauthorized access. Organizations that implement robust cryptographic access controls minimize the risk of credential theft, privilege escalation, and unauthorized machine communications.

As enterprises continue to expand their use of machine identities, the cryptographic foundations that support them must remain strong and adaptable to evolving threats. A combination of secure authentication methods, encryption protocols, key management practices, certificate governance, and emerging quantum-resistant technologies forms the backbone of a resilient machine identity security strategy. Organizations that invest in cryptographic best practices not only protect their machine identities from compromise but also ensure the integrity, confidentiality, and availability of their critical digital assets in an increasingly interconnected world.

Digital Certificates and Their Role in Machine Identity

Digital certificates are a fundamental component of machine identity management, providing a secure mechanism for authenticating machines, encrypting communications, and ensuring the integrity of interactions between non-human entities. As enterprises increasingly rely on cloud environments, microservices, and automated workflows, the need for secure machine-to-machine authentication has become more critical than ever. Digital certificates serve as cryptographic credentials that verify the legitimacy of machine identities, allowing applications, servers, APIs, and devices to establish trusted connections in enterprise environments. Without properly managed digital certificates, organizations face significant security risks, including unauthorized access, identity spoofing, and data interception.

At the core of digital certificates is the principle of public key infrastructure (PKI), which provides a framework for issuing, managing, and revoking certificates. A digital certificate consists of a public key, associated metadata, and a cryptographic signature from a trusted certificate authority (CA). The CA acts as a central authority that validates the authenticity of machine identities and ensures that only authorized systems can obtain certificates. By signing a certificate with its private key, the CA guarantees that the entity presenting the certificate is legitimate. The recipient of a digital certificate can verify its authenticity by checking the CA's digital signature, ensuring that the identity is not forged or compromised.

The primary function of digital certificates in machine identity management is authentication. In modern enterprise environments, machines must authenticate themselves before initiating secure communications. When a machine presents a valid certificate, it proves its identity to the requesting entity, establishing a trust relationship. This process is particularly important in cloud services, where virtual machines, containers, and applications interact dynamically across distributed networks. Digital certificates eliminate the need for static credentials such as passwords or API keys, reducing the risk of credential theft and unauthorized access. By enforcing certificate-based authentication, enterprises ensure that only trusted machines can communicate with sensitive systems and resources.

Encryption is another critical role of digital certificates in machine identity security. When two machines communicate, they must encrypt their data to prevent unauthorized parties from intercepting or tampering with the information. Digital certificates facilitate this process by enabling the use of secure communication protocols such as Transport Layer Security (TLS). In a TLS handshake, two machines exchange certificates, verify each other's identities, and establish an encrypted communication channel. This process protects sensitive data from eavesdropping and man-in-the-middle attacks, ensuring that information remains confidential throughout its transmission. The strength of the encryption depends on the cryptographic algorithms used, with modern certificates employing elliptic curve cryptography (ECC) and advanced RSA key pairs to enhance security.

Integrity verification is another essential function of digital certificates in machine identity management. When a machine transmits data, the recipient must ensure that the information has not been altered or tampered with during transmission. Digital certificates incorporate cryptographic hashing techniques that generate unique signatures for transmitted messages. If an attacker attempts to modify the data, the signature will no longer match, alerting the recipient to potential manipulation. This mechanism ensures that machine-to-machine communications remain trustworthy and that no unauthorized modifications have been made. Integrity verification is particularly critical in financial transactions, software distribution, and secure API communications, where data integrity directly impacts business operations.

Certificate lifecycle management is a crucial aspect of maintaining a secure machine identity environment. Digital certificates have expiration dates, and failing to renew them in time can cause service disruptions, broken authentication mechanisms, and security vulnerabilities. Enterprises must implement automated certificate management solutions to track expiration dates, issue timely renewals, and revoke compromised certificates when necessary. Without proper lifecycle management, expired or misconfigured certificates can lead to system downtime, creating operational and security risks. Automated renewal processes help organizations avoid unexpected failures and maintain continuous security coverage for their machine identities.

Certificate revocation is another key function of digital certificates in machine identity security. When a certificate is compromised, lost, or no longer needed, it must be revoked to prevent unauthorized use. Certificate authorities maintain Certificate Revocation Lists (CRLs) and Online Certificate Status Protocol (OCSP) services that allow machines to check the validity of a certificate in real time. If a certificate is found on a revocation list, it is deemed untrustworthy, preventing its further use in authentication or encryption processes. Enterprises must ensure that revoked certificates are promptly removed from their environments to prevent attackers from using stolen or outdated credentials to gain access to sensitive systems.

The growing complexity of machine identities has increased the demand for scalable certificate management solutions. Large enterprises manage thousands, if not millions, of machine identities, making manual certificate administration impractical. Certificate automation platforms integrate with existing identity and access management (IAM) systems to streamline the issuance, renewal, and revocation of digital certificates. These platforms provide centralized visibility, enforce security policies, and reduce the risk of human errors that could lead to misconfigured certificates or expired credentials. Automated certificate management improves security posture, enhances operational efficiency, and ensures compliance with industry regulations.

Regulatory and compliance frameworks emphasize the importance of securing digital certificates in machine identity management. Standards such as GDPR, HIPAA, PCI-DSS, and NIST require organizations to implement strong encryption mechanisms, authenticate machine identities, and maintain secure communication channels. Digital certificates play a central role in meeting these requirements by providing cryptographic assurance that machine identities are legitimate and that transmitted data is protected. Enterprises that fail to properly manage their certificates may face regulatory fines, security breaches, and reputational damage. Adhering to industry standards helps organizations mitigate risks and demonstrate compliance with security best practices.

As cyber threats continue to evolve, the role of digital certificates in machine identity management will become even more critical. Attackers constantly seek ways to exploit weak authentication mechanisms, intercept sensitive data, and impersonate trusted systems. Organizations must stay ahead of these threats by implementing robust certificate management strategies, enforcing security policies, and leveraging automation to maintain control over their machine identities. By securing digital certificates and integrating them into a comprehensive identity management framework, enterprises can strengthen their overall security posture and protect their digital assets from emerging cyber risks.

Public Key Infrastructure (PKI) and Machine Identities

Public Key Infrastructure (PKI) is a foundational security framework that enables authentication, encryption, and digital signature verification for both human and machine identities. In the context of machine identity management, PKI provides the necessary cryptographic mechanisms to establish trust between applications, cloud workloads, APIs, IoT devices, and other non-human entities. As enterprises increasingly rely on automated and interconnected systems, securing machine identities through PKI has become essential for preventing unauthorized access, securing communications, and ensuring data integrity. Without a properly managed PKI, machine identities become vulnerable to exploitation, leading to identity spoofing, man-in-the-middle attacks, and unauthorized system access.

At its core, PKI is based on asymmetric cryptography, which involves a pair of keys: a public key and a private key. These keys work together to enable secure authentication and encryption. The public key is shared openly and used to encrypt data, while the private key is kept secret and used for decryption. In machine identity management, PKI enables systems to authenticate each other by verifying digital certificates that bind public keys to specific machine entities. This trust mechanism ensures that only authorized machines can communicate within an enterprise network, reducing the risk of impersonation attacks and unauthorized access.

A key component of PKI is the certificate authority (CA), which is responsible for issuing, validating, and revoking digital certificates. The CA acts as a trusted entity that vouches for the authenticity of machine identities by signing certificates with its private key. When a machine presents a digital certificate, other systems verify its legitimacy by checking the CA's signature against the CA's public key. This validation process ensures that machine identities cannot be forged or manipulated by malicious actors. Enterprises often operate their own internal CAs to issue and manage machine identity certificates, while also relying on external CAs for public-facing services.

Certificate issuance within PKI follows a structured process to ensure the legitimacy of machine identities. When a new machine, application, or service requires authentication, it generates a key pair and submits a certificate signing request (CSR) to the CA. The CSR contains the machine's public key and identity information. The CA then verifies the request, signs the certificate, and issues it to the machine. This certificate serves as proof of identity, allowing the machine to authenticate itself securely in encrypted transactions. Properly managing the certificate issuance process is crucial to preventing unauthorized machines from obtaining trusted credentials.

PKI also includes certificate revocation mechanisms to handle situations where machine identities become compromised, outdated, or no longer needed. When a certificate is revoked, it is added to a Certificate Revocation List (CRL) or an Online Certificate Status Protocol (OCSP) responder. Machines checking the validity of certificates can query these revocation lists to ensure that the credentials they are trusting have not been revoked due to a security breach or expiration. Regularly updating and monitoring revoked certificates prevents attackers from using compromised machine identities to gain unauthorized access.

The lifecycle management of machine identity certificates is a critical aspect of PKI implementation. Digital certificates have predefined expiration dates to prevent their indefinite use, reducing the risk of security vulnerabilities associated with outdated credentials. When a certificate reaches its expiration date, it must be renewed to maintain secure authentication and encryption. Enterprises that fail to track certificate expiration dates risk operational disruptions, as expired certificates can lead to broken authentication mechanisms, system outages, and insecure communications. Automated certificate lifecycle management tools help organizations streamline renewal processes, ensuring that machine identities remain continuously protected.

Encryption is a fundamental function of PKI, providing confidentiality for data transmitted between machines. Secure communication protocols such as Transport Layer Security (TLS) rely on PKI-based certificates to establish encrypted connections. When a machine initiates a TLS handshake, it presents its certificate to the recipient, which verifies its authenticity before establishing a secure session. This encryption process prevents attackers from intercepting or altering sensitive data in transit. Proper PKI implementation ensures that only strong encryption algorithms are used, reducing the risk of cryptographic weaknesses that could be exploited by cybercriminals.

PKI also supports digital signatures, which are essential for ensuring the integrity and authenticity of machine-generated data. When a machine signs a message or transaction with its private key, the recipient can verify the signature using the corresponding public key. This process confirms that the data has not been altered and that it originates from a legitimate source. Digital signatures are widely used in software updates, secure API communications, and cryptographic attestations, providing an additional layer of trust for machine identities. By leveraging PKI for digital signatures, enterprises can prevent unauthorized modifications to critical data and applications.

The complexity of managing PKI at scale has led organizations to adopt automated PKI solutions that integrate with identity and access management (IAM) systems. As enterprises deploy thousands or even millions of machine identities across cloud environments, microservices architectures, and hybrid infrastructures, manual certificate management becomes impractical. Automated PKI platforms streamline certificate issuance, renewal, revocation, and monitoring, reducing administrative overhead while ensuring security best practices are consistently applied. By centralizing PKI operations, organizations gain better visibility and control over their machine identity landscape.

PKI governance and compliance play a significant role in ensuring that machine identity management aligns with industry regulations and security policies. Standards such as GDPR, HIPAA, PCI-DSS, and NIST require enterprises to implement strong encryption, certificate-based authentication, and proper key management practices. Adhering to these regulatory frameworks helps organizations protect sensitive data, prevent security breaches, and demonstrate compliance during audits. PKI governance frameworks define policies for certificate issuance, usage, and expiration, ensuring that machine identities are managed in accordance with security best practices.

As cyber threats evolve, the role of PKI in securing machine identities will continue to grow. Attackers frequently target weakly protected certificates, exploit expired credentials, and intercept insecure communications to compromise enterprise systems. Organizations must remain proactive in implementing robust PKI policies, enforcing automated certificate management, and continuously monitoring the integrity of their machine identities. Strengthening PKI practices enhances enterprise security, safeguards sensitive data, and ensures that machine-to-machine interactions remain trustworthy in an increasingly digital and automated world.

Secure Key Management Practices

Key management is a fundamental aspect of machine identity security, ensuring that cryptographic keys used for authentication, encryption, and digital signatures are protected from unauthorized access and misuse. As enterprises increasingly rely on machine identities to secure cloud workloads, applications, and automated systems, implementing secure key management practices becomes essential. The strength of any cryptographic system is only as good as the security of its keys. Poor key management can lead to breaches, identity compromise, and operational disruptions. Organizations must establish a structured approach to generating, storing, rotating, and revoking cryptographic keys to maintain trust in their digital infrastructure.

The foundation of secure key management begins with proper key generation. Cryptographic keys must be generated using strong algorithms and sufficient entropy to prevent predictability. Weak keys or those generated using insufficient randomness are susceptible to brute-force attacks, allowing adversaries to compromise encrypted communications and machine identities. Organizations should use hardware security modules (HSMs) or dedicated key management systems (KMS) to generate and store keys securely. These systems provide a controlled environment that protects keys from unauthorized access, reducing the risk of theft or exposure. Ensuring that all keys adhere to modern cryptographic standards such as RSA-4096, ECC-256, and AES-256 strengthens machine identity security.

Storing cryptographic keys securely is critical to preventing unauthorized access and misuse. Keys should never be hardcoded into application source code, stored in plaintext files, or embedded within configuration settings. Attackers frequently scan code repositories, logs, and publicly exposed assets for hardcoded keys, which can lead to security breaches if discovered. Instead, organizations should use secrets management solutions and dedicated key vaults to store and manage cryptographic keys securely. Cloud providers offer managed key vaults that integrate with identity and access management systems, allowing organizations to control access to keys based on strict security policies. Proper access control mechanisms ensure that only authorized applications and services can retrieve and use cryptographic keys.

Key rotation is a crucial practice in mitigating the risk of key compromise. The longer a key remains in use, the greater the risk that it may be exposed or compromised. Regularly rotating encryption keys, API keys, and authentication credentials reduces the impact of potential breaches by limiting the time window during which a compromised key can be used. Automated key rotation mechanisms help organizations enforce best practices by replacing keys on a scheduled basis without disrupting operations. When rotating keys, enterprises must ensure that all dependent systems are updated with the new credentials to prevent service disruptions or authentication failures. Implementing rolling key updates ensures continuous security while maintaining seamless system functionality.

Key access controls define which users, applications, and systems have permission to access or use cryptographic keys. Enforcing the principle of least privilege ensures that only authorized entities can retrieve or manipulate keys, reducing the risk of insider threats and unauthorized access. Role-based access control (RBAC) and attribute-based access control (ABAC) mechanisms should be implemented to restrict key usage based on predefined security policies. Logging and monitoring access to cryptographic keys provide visibility into key usage, allowing security teams to detect anomalies or unauthorized access attempts. Regular audits of key permissions help organizations identify and remove unnecessary access, minimizing security risks.

Key revocation and decommissioning ensure that compromised or unused keys do not pose a security threat. When a cryptographic key is suspected to be compromised or is no longer needed, it must be revoked and replaced immediately. Key management systems provide mechanisms for revoking keys and issuing new ones without disrupting operations. Revoked keys should be securely deleted to prevent their retrieval and reuse. In environments where multiple systems rely on a single key, proper decommissioning processes must be followed to ensure that outdated keys are no longer in use. Enterprises should establish policies that define when and how keys should be retired from active service, preventing unauthorized use of legacy credentials.

Secure transmission of cryptographic keys is essential to preventing interception by malicious actors. When distributing keys between systems, organizations must use encrypted channels such as TLS or secure key exchange protocols like Diffie-Hellman and Elliptic Curve Diffie-Hellman (ECDH). Transmitting keys in plaintext over unencrypted networks exposes them to attackers who can intercept and misuse them. Secure key exchange protocols ensure that keys are shared only between trusted parties without exposure to intermediaries. In scenarios where keys must be transferred between cloud environments, organizations should use secure envelope encryption techniques to wrap keys in additional layers of protection.

Key backup and recovery strategies safeguard against data loss and accidental key deletion. Cryptographic keys play a critical role in securing encrypted data, and losing access to them can result in permanent data loss. Organizations must implement secure backup procedures that store copies of encryption keys in protected environments separate from production systems. Key backups should be encrypted and access-controlled to prevent unauthorized retrieval. Disaster recovery plans should include key restoration processes that enable rapid key recovery in case of failures, system crashes, or cyberattacks. Ensuring that backup copies are regularly updated and securely stored prevents operational disruptions due to lost or inaccessible keys.

Monitoring and logging key usage provide insights into how cryptographic keys are being accessed and used within an organization. Security teams must implement continuous monitoring solutions that track key activity, detect anomalies, and generate alerts for suspicious behavior. Unusual patterns, such as frequent key access from unknown locations or repeated failed decryption attempts, may indicate a security breach. Integrating key management logs with security information and event management (SIEM) systems enhances threat detection capabilities, allowing organizations to respond to potential compromises in real time. Regular security audits help validate key management practices, ensuring that compliance requirements are met and security risks are minimized.

The increasing complexity of enterprise security environments has driven the need for automation in key management. Manual key management processes introduce risks such as misconfigurations, human errors, and inconsistent enforcement of security policies. Automated key management solutions streamline the process of generating, storing, rotating, and revoking keys, ensuring that best practices are consistently applied across all systems. Integration with cloud-native security services, DevOps pipelines, and identity management platforms enhances security by enforcing uniform key policies across distributed environments. Organizations that leverage automation reduce the risk of key exposure while improving operational efficiency and security resilience.

As enterprises expand their use of machine identities, implementing secure key management practices is essential to maintaining a strong security posture. The effectiveness of cryptographic systems depends on the ability to protect, control, and monitor the lifecycle of encryption keys. Organizations must adopt a comprehensive approach that includes strong key generation, secure storage, regular rotation, strict access controls, effective revocation mechanisms, and automated management solutions. By enforcing these best practices, enterprises can mitigate security risks, prevent unauthorized access, and ensure the integrity of their machine identities in an increasingly interconnected digital landscape.

The Role of Certificate Authorities in Machine Identity

Certificate Authorities (CAs) play a fundamental role in machine identity management by acting as trusted entities that issue, validate, and revoke digital certificates. These certificates are essential for authenticating machines, encrypting communications, and ensuring the integrity of interactions between non-human entities such as applications, cloud services, IoT devices, and APIs. Without a reliable CA infrastructure, machine identities would lack a verifiable mechanism to establish trust, leaving enterprises vulnerable to identity spoofing, unauthorized access, and man-in-the-middle attacks. As organizations increasingly rely on automation, cloud computing, and interconnected digital services, the role of CAs in securing machine identities has become more critical than ever.

A CA is responsible for issuing digital certificates that bind a machine's public key to its identity. This process involves verifying the legitimacy of the machine requesting a certificate and then digitally signing the issued certificate using the CA's private key. The signed certificate serves as proof that the machine is trustworthy and that its public key can be used for secure communication. Other machines or systems that receive the certificate can verify its authenticity by checking the CA's digital signature against the CA's public key, ensuring that the identity being presented is legitimate. The CA effectively acts as a trusted third party that establishes confidence in machine identities across distributed environments.

The certificate issuance process follows a structured approach to ensure the security and legitimacy of machine identities. When a machine or service requires a certificate, it generates a key pair consisting of a public key and a private key. The public key is included in a Certificate Signing Request (CSR), which is then submitted to the CA. The CA reviews the request, verifies the machine's identity, and signs the certificate using its private key. Once issued, the certificate is deployed to the machine, allowing it to authenticate itself and establish encrypted connections. Properly managing this issuance process is crucial to preventing unauthorized machines from obtaining valid certificates that could be used for malicious purposes.

CAs also play a critical role in certificate validation, ensuring that machine identities remain trustworthy throughout their lifecycle. When a machine presents a certificate during authentication, the receiving system checks the certificate chain to verify its authenticity. The certificate chain consists of the machine's certificate, any intermediate certificates, and the CA's root certificate. If any certificate in the chain is invalid, expired, or revoked, the authentication process fails, preventing the machine from establishing a secure connection. This validation mechanism helps protect enterprises from unauthorized entities attempting to use fraudulent certificates to gain access to sensitive systems.

Certificate revocation is another essential function of CAs, allowing enterprises to invalidate certificates that have been compromised, lost, or are no longer needed. When a certificate is revoked, it is added to a Certificate Revocation List (CRL) or marked as invalid using the Online Certificate Status Protocol (OCSP). Machines checking the validity of a certificate can query these revocation lists to determine whether the certificate should be trusted. Revoking certificates promptly ensures that attackers cannot use stolen or misconfigured credentials to impersonate legitimate machines. Organizations must implement automated revocation processes to ensure that compromised certificates are deactivated without delay.

Managing the lifecycle of machine identity certificates is a key responsibility of CAs. Digital certificates have expiration dates to prevent their indefinite use, reducing the risk of security vulnerabilities associated with outdated credentials. When a certificate approaches its expiration date, it must be renewed to maintain secure authentication and encryption. Enterprises that fail to track certificate expiration dates risk operational disruptions, as expired certificates can lead to broken authentication mechanisms, service outages, and security gaps. Automated certificate lifecycle management solutions help organizations streamline renewals, ensuring that machine identities remain continuously protected and operational.

The choice between using public and private CAs depends on an enterprise's security requirements and operational needs. Public CAs, such as DigiCert, GlobalSign, and Let's Encrypt, provide certificates that are widely recognized and trusted across different networks, making them suitable for external-facing applications, websites, and APIs. Private CAs, on the other hand, are deployed within an organization's internal infrastructure to issue certificates for internal systems, cloud workloads, and machine-to-machine authentication. While public CAs offer convenience and global trust, private CAs provide greater control over certificate issuance policies, enabling enterprises to enforce stricter security measures for their internal machine identities.

Enterprises operating in highly regulated industries must ensure that their CA operations comply with security standards and best practices. Regulatory frameworks such as GDPR, HIPAA, PCI-DSS, and NIST mandate the use of strong encryption, certificate-based authentication, and proper key management practices to protect sensitive data. Adhering to these standards helps organizations mitigate security risks and demonstrate compliance during audits. CA governance frameworks define policies for certificate issuance, usage, and expiration, ensuring that machine identities are managed in accordance with security best practices.

CAs also play a vital role in securing cloud environments, where machine identities are frequently generated and decommissioned. Cloud providers such as AWS, Microsoft Azure, and Google Cloud offer integrated CA services that enable enterprises to automate certificate issuance and management across distributed cloud infrastructures. These cloud-based CA solutions provide scalable, policy-driven approaches to machine identity security, reducing administrative overhead while maintaining robust authentication and encryption mechanisms. Integrating cloud CA services with identity and access management (IAM) platforms further enhances security by ensuring that machine identities follow the same governance principles as human identities.

Threat actors frequently target CAs as a means of undermining machine identity security. A compromised CA can issue fraudulent certificates, allowing attackers to impersonate legitimate machines, intercept encrypted communications, and bypass security controls. To mitigate this risk, organizations must implement strict access controls, multi-factor authentication, and hardware security modules (HSMs) to protect CA private keys. Regular security audits, monitoring of certificate issuance activity, and continuous vulnerability assessments help detect and prevent CA-related security threats. Organizations that operate their own private CAs must enforce strong operational security measures to maintain trust in their machine identity ecosystem.

As machine identities continue to proliferate across enterprise networks, the role of CAs in securing digital interactions will only become more critical. Attackers are constantly evolving their tactics to exploit weak authentication mechanisms, intercept sensitive data, and impersonate trusted systems. Organizations must remain vigilant in implementing robust CA policies, automating certificate lifecycle management, and continuously monitoring the integrity of issued certificates. By strengthening CA security practices, enterprises can protect their machine identities, ensure secure communication, and build a resilient digital infrastructure in an increasingly complex cybersecurity landscape.

Authentication and Authorization for Machines

As enterprises expand their digital ecosystems, the need for robust authentication and authorization mechanisms for machines has become critical. Unlike human users, machines—including applications, cloud workloads, APIs, IoT devices, and automated scripts—must authenticate themselves to access systems, transmit data, and execute tasks securely. Machine authentication ensures that only verified and trusted entities can communicate within an enterprise network, while authorization defines what actions they are permitted to perform. Without strong authentication and authorization controls, organizations risk security breaches, identity spoofing, data leaks, and privilege escalation attacks that could compromise sensitive information and disrupt business operations.

Machine authentication is the process of verifying a machine's identity before granting access to a system or resource. Unlike human authentication, which typically relies on usernames, passwords, and multi-factor authentication, machine authentication uses cryptographic credentials such as digital certificates, API keys, SSH keys, and secure tokens. Digital certificates, issued through public key infrastructure (PKI), allow machines to authenticate themselves by presenting a valid certificate that proves their identity. When a machine initiates a connection, it presents its certificate to the receiving system, which verifies its authenticity by checking the certificate's digital signature against a trusted certificate authority (CA). If the certificate is valid and has not expired or been revoked, authentication is granted, allowing the machine to proceed with the interaction.

API keys are another widely used method of machine authentication, enabling secure communication between applications and services. When an API request is made, the requesting machine must include a valid API key in the request header to authenticate itself. API keys act as unique identifiers that verify the legitimacy of the requesting entity. However, API keys must be securely managed to prevent unauthorized access. Hardcoding API keys in source code, storing them in plaintext files, or exposing them in public repositories increases the risk of key theft. Organizations must implement best practices such as storing API keys in secure vaults, enforcing access controls, and rotating keys periodically to minimize security risks.

OAuth and OpenID Connect are widely adopted authentication frameworks that enable machines to obtain access tokens for secure authentication. OAuth allows machines to authenticate using authorization tokens instead of static credentials. A machine requesting access to a resource receives a token from an authorization server, which grants temporary access based on predefined security policies. OpenID Connect extends OAuth by providing identity verification capabilities, ensuring that machines not only authenticate securely but also establish trust with other systems. These authentication protocols enhance security by eliminating the need for static credentials while providing granular access control mechanisms.

Beyond authentication, machine authorization determines the level of access a machine has within an enterprise system. Authorization policies define which machines can access specific data, perform certain operations, and interact with restricted resources. Without proper authorization enforcement, authenticated machines could gain excessive privileges, leading to security vulnerabilities such as unauthorized data exposure, privilege escalation, and potential misuse of system resources. Role-based access control (RBAC) and attribute-based access control (ABAC) frameworks provide structured approaches to enforcing machine authorization, ensuring that each machine operates within the least privilege model.

RBAC assigns access permissions based on predefined roles, grouping machines into categories such as service accounts, application workloads, or API consumers. Each role is associated with specific permissions that define what actions the machine can perform. For example, a machine acting as a database server may only be allowed to read and write data but not modify system configurations. By implementing RBAC, enterprises can prevent machines from accessing unauthorized resources, reducing the risk of privilege escalation attacks.

ABAC extends RBAC by incorporating additional attributes such as environment variables, device type, geolocation, and time-based access conditions. In an ABAC model, access decisions are dynamically evaluated based on a combination of identity attributes and contextual information. For instance, an IoT device may be granted access to a cloud service only if it is operating within a predefined geographical region and using an approved security configuration. ABAC provides more fine-grained control over machine authorization, ensuring that security policies adapt to real-time conditions.

Zero trust security models emphasize the importance of strong authentication and authorization for machines by enforcing continuous verification. In a zero trust architecture, no machine is inherently trusted, and access is granted based on strict identity verification and policy enforcement. Machines must authenticate themselves at every interaction, and authorization policies are continuously evaluated to ensure that access remains appropriate. Zero trust principles mitigate risks such as lateral movement within a network, ensuring that even if one machine is compromised, attackers cannot gain unrestricted access to other systems.

Machine-to-machine authentication and authorization also play a crucial role in cloud environments, where workloads and services interact dynamically. Cloud platforms provide identity and access management (IAM) solutions that govern how machines authenticate and what resources they can access. IAM policies allow enterprises to define machine identity permissions, restricting access based on security requirements. Cloud-native security tools, such as AWS IAM roles, Azure Managed Identities, and Google Cloud Service Accounts, provide automated mechanisms for managing machine access without exposing sensitive credentials. Properly configuring IAM policies ensures that cloud-based machine identities adhere to the same security standards as on-premises systems.

Monitoring and auditing machine authentication and authorization events are essential for detecting anomalies and preventing security incidents. Enterprises must implement logging mechanisms that track authentication attempts, failed access requests, and privilege changes for machine identities. Security information and event management (SIEM) systems aggregate logs from various sources, analyzing patterns to identify potential threats. If an unauthorized machine attempts to authenticate or a machine unexpectedly requests elevated permissions, security teams can respond proactively to mitigate the risk. Regular audits of machine identity policies help organizations identify misconfigurations, enforce compliance, and strengthen security postures.

Automation is key to managing machine authentication and authorization at scale. As enterprises deploy thousands or even millions of machine identities across cloud environments, microservices architectures, and hybrid infrastructures, manual management becomes impractical. Automated identity orchestration solutions streamline the enforcement of authentication protocols, authorization policies, and credential lifecycle management. Integrating automation with security frameworks ensures that machine identities are dynamically managed, reducing human error and improving operational efficiency.

As machine identities continue to proliferate across enterprise networks, securing their authentication and authorization processes is more important than ever. Attackers actively target weakly protected credentials, exploit misconfigured access policies, and impersonate legitimate machines to infiltrate systems. Organizations must implement robust authentication mechanisms, enforce strict authorization policies, and continuously monitor machine identity activity to mitigate risks. Strengthening machine authentication and authorization practices ensures that enterprise systems remain secure, resilient, and protected against evolving cyber threats.

Zero Trust and Machine Identity Management

Zero Trust is a modern security framework that eliminates implicit trust in any entity, whether human or machine, requiring continuous verification and strict access controls for every interaction within an enterprise network. Traditional security models operated under the assumption that once inside a corporate perimeter, machines and users could be trusted to access resources. However, with the increasing sophistication of cyber threats, cloud adoption, remote work, and the proliferation of machine identities, organizations have recognized the necessity of shifting to a Zero Trust architecture. Machine identity management plays a crucial role in this framework by ensuring that all machines—whether applications, workloads, APIs, IoT devices, or cloud services—are authenticated, authorized, and continuously monitored for suspicious activity.

The foundation of Zero Trust is built on the principle of never assuming trust, requiring every machine to authenticate itself before being granted access. This approach significantly reduces the risk of lateral movement within a network, as even compromised machines are unable to access other systems without proper authentication and authorization. Machine identities serve as digital credentials that

45

enable machines to verify themselves using cryptographic methods such as digital certificates, secure tokens, and cryptographic key pairs. Unlike traditional network security models that rely on static credentials and perimeter defenses, Zero Trust dynamically enforces authentication at every interaction, ensuring that machine identities remain secure at all times.

Machine authentication in a Zero Trust model requires strong identity verification mechanisms. Public Key Infrastructure (PKI) plays a fundamental role in this process by enabling certificate-based authentication, ensuring that only machines with valid digital certificates can communicate within an enterprise environment. Certificates issued by trusted certificate authorities (CAs) bind a machine's identity to its public key, allowing other machines to verify its authenticity before exchanging data. By enforcing certificate-based authentication, organizations eliminate the risks associated with weak credentials, reducing the likelihood of machine identity compromise.

Beyond authentication, Zero Trust mandates strict authorization policies that define what actions a machine can perform once authenticated. Machine authorization follows the principle of least privilege, granting machines only the access necessary to perform their intended functions. Role-based access control (RBAC) and attribute-based access control (ABAC) frameworks help enforce fine-grained authorization policies, ensuring that machines cannot escalate privileges or access unauthorized resources. In a Zero Trust environment, access decisions are continuously evaluated based on factors such as machine identity, security posture, environmental context, and real-time threat intelligence. This adaptive approach minimizes security risks by ensuring that machine access permissions align with evolving security policies.

Zero Trust also requires continuous monitoring of machine identities to detect anomalous behavior and potential threats. Traditional security models often relied on one-time authentication, assuming that once a machine was verified, it could maintain access indefinitely. However, attackers who gain control of a legitimate machine identity can exploit this trust to move undetected within a network. Zero Trust counters this risk by enforcing continuous authentication, validating machine identities at every transaction, session, or interaction.

Security teams leverage telemetry data, behavioral analytics, and artificial intelligence to identify deviations from normal machine behavior, triggering alerts or automated responses when suspicious activity is detected.

In cloud environments, Zero Trust principles are essential for securing machine identities across distributed and dynamic infrastructures. Cloud workloads frequently interact with APIs, containers, and serverless functions, making identity management more complex than traditional on-premises systems. Cloud providers offer identity and access management (IAM) solutions that integrate Zero Trust principles, enforcing strict authentication and authorization controls for machine identities. Solutions such as AWS IAM roles, Azure Managed Identities, and Google Cloud Service Accounts provide dynamic identity management for cloud-based machines, ensuring that access is continuously evaluated based on Zero Trust policies.

Zero Trust also strengthens machine-to-machine communication security by enforcing encryption and secure connectivity. Machine identities play a key role in establishing encrypted connections using protocols such as Transport Layer Security (TLS). In a Zero Trust model, machines must authenticate themselves using digital certificates before initiating any communication, ensuring that data exchanges occur only between verified and authorized entities. Mutual TLS (mTLS) further enhances security by requiring both communicating machines to authenticate each other, preventing unauthorized systems from intercepting or tampering with encrypted data. By enforcing encrypted machine-to-machine communication, organizations reduce the risk of man-in-the-middle attacks and data exfiltration.

One of the biggest challenges in adopting Zero Trust for machine identity management is the scale and complexity of modern enterprise environments. Organizations must manage thousands or even millions of machine identities across cloud, hybrid, and on-premises infrastructures. Manual identity management processes are insufficient to enforce Zero Trust principles effectively, making automation a necessity. Automated identity orchestration solutions streamline the issuance, renewal, and revocation of digital certificates, API keys, and cryptographic secrets. These solutions integrate with existing security frameworks, ensuring that machine identities comply with Zero Trust policies without introducing operational bottlenecks.

Zero Trust also requires organizations to implement policy-driven security controls that adapt to real-time risk assessments. Static access control lists and pre-defined permissions are no longer sufficient in an era of dynamic threats and evolving attack vectors. Organizations must adopt policy enforcement engines that evaluate security conditions continuously, granting or revoking machine access based on contextual factors such as location, behavioral patterns, and security posture. By leveraging Zero Trust network access (ZTNA) technologies, enterprises can enforce identity-based segmentation, isolating machines from unauthorized resources and limiting the blast radius of potential security incidents.

Compliance and regulatory requirements further highlight the importance of Zero Trust in machine identity management. Data protection regulations such as GDPR, HIPAA, PCI-DSS, and NIST mandate strict identity verification, encryption, and access control measures to protect sensitive information. Zero Trust provides a framework that aligns with these regulatory standards by ensuring that machine identities undergo rigorous authentication and authorization processes. Implementing Zero Trust principles helps organizations meet compliance obligations while reducing the risk of data breaches and unauthorized access.

Organizations that embrace Zero Trust for machine identity management gain a significant security advantage by eliminating implicit trust, enforcing continuous verification, and dynamically adapting to emerging threats. As cyberattacks become more sophisticated, traditional perimeter-based security models are no longer sufficient to protect enterprise systems. Zero Trust provides a proactive approach that secures machine identities at every level, ensuring that access is granted based on verified trust rather than static credentials. By integrating Zero Trust principles into machine identity management strategies, enterprises can enhance security, improve resilience, and protect their digital ecosystems from evolving cyber threats.

The Lifecycle of Machine Identities

Machine identities play a crucial role in securing modern digital environments, enabling authentication, encryption, and trusted communication between non-human entities such as applications, APIs, cloud workloads, IoT devices, and automated processes. Unlike human identities, which remain relatively stable over time, machine identities have a dynamic lifecycle that involves multiple phases, from creation to decommissioning. Each stage of this lifecycle requires strict management and security controls to prevent unauthorized access, identity sprawl, and exploitation by malicious actors. Without a structured approach to lifecycle management, organizations risk losing visibility over machine identities, leading to security vulnerabilities, operational disruptions, and compliance violations.

The lifecycle of a machine identity begins with its creation, where a unique identifier is assigned to a machine or service. This process typically involves generating cryptographic credentials such as digital certificates, API keys, SSH keys, or cryptographic tokens. The identity issuance process must follow strict security policies to ensure that only authorized machines receive valid credentials. For certificate-based authentication, a machine generates a key pair and submits a certificate signing request (CSR) to a trusted certificate authority (CA). Once verified, the CA issues a digital certificate, binding the machine's identity to its public key. This certificate acts as proof of authenticity, allowing the machine to establish secure connections with other systems.

Once issued, a machine identity enters the operational phase, where it is actively used for authentication and authorization. During this stage, machine identities enable secure communication between applications, enforce access controls, and facilitate encrypted transactions. Identity governance mechanisms ensure that each machine identity operates within defined security policies, preventing unauthorized privilege escalation. Role-based access control (RBAC) and attribute-based access control (ABAC) frameworks help restrict machine access to only necessary resources, following the principle of least privilege. Continuous monitoring is essential during this phase to detect anomalies, prevent misuse, and ensure that machine identities function as intended.

Key rotation and renewal are critical processes in the lifecycle of a machine identity. Over time, cryptographic keys and certificates must be rotated to reduce the risk of compromise and maintain security best practices. If a machine identity relies on static credentials that never change, attackers who gain access to these credentials can use them indefinitely, posing a significant security threat. Automated key rotation policies ensure that cryptographic credentials are refreshed regularly, limiting the exposure of compromised keys. Certificate renewal processes prevent service disruptions by replacing expiring certificates with new ones before they become invalid. Organizations that fail to implement automated renewal mechanisms risk unexpected outages when expired certificates cause authentication failures and broken communications.

Machine identity revocation becomes necessary when an identity is compromised, no longer needed, or reaches the end of its intended use. When a certificate, API key, or cryptographic credential is revoked, it is invalidated, preventing unauthorized systems from using it for authentication. Certificate authorities maintain certificate revocation lists (CRLs) and Online Certificate Status Protocol (OCSP) services that allow other machines to check the validity of certificates in real-time. Revocation processes must be swift and automated to ensure that compromised identities cannot be exploited for extended periods. Organizations that do not enforce proper revocation policies risk allowing attackers to use stolen credentials even after they have been decommissioned.

Decommissioning is the final stage in the lifecycle of a machine identity, marking its permanent removal from an organization's identity ecosystem. When a machine or service is retired, its associated credentials must be securely deleted to prevent unauthorized access. Decommissioning also involves updating identity inventories and revoking unused credentials to prevent orphaned machine identities from lingering in the system. Orphaned identities—those that are no longer associated with an active system but still retain valid credentials—pose a significant security risk, as attackers can exploit them to gain unauthorized access. Properly decommissioning machine identities ensures that organizations maintain a clean and secure identity environment, reducing the attack surface and preventing credential misuse.

Auditing and compliance play a crucial role throughout the lifecycle of machine identities, ensuring that identity management processes align with security policies and regulatory requirements. Organizations operating in highly regulated industries must demonstrate compliance with frameworks such as GDPR, HIPAA, PCI-DSS, and NIST, which mandate strict identity governance, encryption, and authentication practices. Regular audits help identify mismanaged identities, detect policy violations, and improve overall security posture. Implementing automated reporting mechanisms provides visibility into the status of machine identities, helping security teams maintain control over their digital infrastructure.

Automation is essential for managing the lifecycle of machine identities at scale. Enterprises dealing with thousands or millions of machine identities cannot rely on manual processes to track issuance, rotation, renewal, and revocation. Automated identity orchestration solutions streamline identity lifecycle management, reducing human error and ensuring consistency in policy enforcement. Integration with identity and access management (IAM) platforms, cloud security tools, and certificate management systems allows organizations to maintain centralized visibility and control over machine identities. By leveraging automation, enterprises can enforce identity best practices, detect anomalies in real time, and respond to security threats more effectively.

The rapid growth of machine identities in cloud environments, microservices architectures, and DevOps workflows has made lifecycle management more complex. DevOps teams frequently deploy and decommission containers, serverless functions, and cloud workloads, generating machine identities that may exist only for minutes or hours. Traditional identity management approaches struggle to keep pace with this ephemeral nature, requiring adaptive lifecycle policies that align with dynamic infrastructure. Short-lived certificates, just-in-time credentials, and temporary access tokens help secure transient machine identities without introducing long-term security risks. Organizations that embrace automated lifecycle management for cloud-native environments can prevent identity sprawl, enforce security controls, and maintain compliance with evolving regulatory requirements.

Threat actors increasingly target machine identities as a means of infiltrating enterprise networks, stealing data, and executing cyberattacks. Weak lifecycle management practices, such as failing to revoke expired credentials or leaving orphaned identities unmanaged, create opportunities for attackers to exploit identity vulnerabilities. Organizations must adopt a proactive approach to machine identity security by enforcing lifecycle best practices, continuously monitoring credential usage, and integrating identity intelligence into their security operations. By strengthening lifecycle management, enterprises can minimize attack surfaces, enhance trust in their digital interactions, and protect their systems from emerging threats.

Machine identities are an integral part of enterprise security, and managing their lifecycle effectively is critical to preventing unauthorized access, identity misuse, and security breaches. Organizations must implement structured lifecycle management frameworks that govern the issuance, use, rotation, revocation, and decommissioning of machine identities. By automating identity lifecycle processes, enforcing strict governance policies, and continuously monitoring identity behavior, enterprises can ensure the security, integrity, and availability of their machine identities in an increasingly complex digital landscape.

Machine Identity Governance and Compliance

Machine identity governance and compliance have become essential components of enterprise security as organizations increasingly rely on digital certificates, cryptographic keys, and authentication tokens to secure machine-to-machine communications. Just as human identities require governance frameworks to manage access rights and ensure compliance with regulatory standards, machine identities must be governed through policies, monitoring, and automation to prevent security risks. Without effective governance, organizations risk identity sprawl, unauthorized access, and compliance violations, leading to potential data breaches and regulatory penalties. Establishing a strong governance model for machine identities ensures that organizations maintain control over their security posture while adhering to industry regulations.

Governance for machine identities involves defining policies and procedures that dictate how identities are issued, used, rotated, and revoked. A structured governance framework ensures that machine identities are managed consistently across an organization, preventing misconfigurations that could lead to security vulnerabilities. Machine identity governance requires visibility into all certificates, API keys, SSH keys, and service accounts used for authentication and encryption. Organizations must implement centralized identity management platforms that provide a comprehensive view of all active machine identities, enabling security teams to detect anomalies, enforce policies, and mitigate risks before they escalate.

One of the primary challenges of machine identity governance is identity sprawl, which occurs when organizations fail to track and manage the growing number of machine identities across their digital environments. With the rise of cloud computing, DevOps automation, and microservices architectures, enterprises now generate machine identities at an unprecedented rate. Each cloud workload, container, and API call may require its own identity, leading to an exponential increase in digital credentials. Without proper governance, machine identities can become orphaned, unmonitored, or misconfigured, increasing the risk of security breaches. Organizations must establish policies that require machine identities to be registered, monitored, and revoked when no longer needed to prevent identity sprawl from becoming a security liability.

Compliance plays a crucial role in machine identity governance, ensuring that organizations adhere to regulatory requirements and industry standards. Regulations such as the General Data Protection Regulation (GDPR), the Health Insurance Portability and Accountability Act (HIPAA), the Payment Card Industry Data Security Standard (PCI-DSS), and the National Institute of Standards and Technology (NIST) Cybersecurity Framework mandate strict controls over authentication, encryption, and access management. Machine identities, which are responsible for securing communications and protecting sensitive data, must comply with these regulations to prevent unauthorized access and data exposure. Failure to enforce compliance with machine identity security requirements can result in legal consequences, financial penalties, and reputational damage.

To meet compliance requirements, organizations must implement auditing and reporting mechanisms that provide visibility into machine identity activity. Security teams must be able to track which machines are using specific certificates, API keys, and authentication credentials, ensuring that access controls are properly enforced. Regular audits help identify unauthorized or misused identities, allowing organizations to take corrective action before security incidents occur. Automated logging solutions integrate with security information and event management (SIEM) systems to collect machine identity activity data, enabling real-time monitoring and alerting for suspicious behavior. By maintaining detailed audit logs, organizations can demonstrate compliance with regulatory frameworks while improving their ability to detect and respond to threats.

Machine identity governance also involves enforcing policy-based controls that define how machine identities should be used and managed. Organizations must establish policies that dictate the minimum security requirements for digital certificates, including key length, expiration periods, and encryption standards. Policies should also specify access control mechanisms, ensuring that machine identities are only granted the permissions necessary for their intended function. Implementing role-based access control (RBAC) and attribute-based access control (ABAC) ensures that machine identities operate under the principle of least privilege, reducing the risk of unauthorized access. Policy enforcement mechanisms help organizations maintain consistency in machine identity security practices while aligning with compliance mandates.

Automation is a critical component of machine identity governance, reducing the complexity of managing thousands or even millions of machine identities across enterprise environments. Manual identity management processes introduce human error and operational inefficiencies, making it difficult to enforce governance at scale. Automated certificate management solutions streamline the issuance, renewal, and revocation of digital certificates, ensuring that machine identities are continuously updated and aligned with security policies. Automated secrets management platforms secure API keys, encryption keys, and SSH credentials, preventing unauthorized access while simplifying compliance with regulatory requirements. By integrating automation into machine identity governance, organizations enhance security, improve operational efficiency, and reduce the risk of credential misuse.

Machine identity governance frameworks must also address the security of third-party integrations and supply chain relationships. Many enterprises rely on external vendors, cloud service providers, and partner organizations that require machine-to-machine communication with internal systems. Without proper governance, third-party machine identities can become security blind spots, exposing enterprises to potential threats such as unauthorized access, data breaches, and supply chain attacks. Organizations must establish strict policies for third-party machine identity management, requiring vendors to follow secure authentication and encryption practices. Continuous monitoring of third-party machine identities ensures that they remain compliant with security policies and do not introduce vulnerabilities into the enterprise network.

Proactive risk management is an essential aspect of machine identity governance, allowing organizations to anticipate and mitigate security threats before they lead to breaches. Security teams must assess the risk associated with machine identities by evaluating their exposure, access permissions, and authentication methods. High-risk machine identities, such as those with elevated privileges or access to sensitive data, require additional security controls such as multi-factor authentication (MFA), short-lived certificates, and just-in-time access policies. Regular risk assessments help organizations prioritize security improvements, ensuring that machine identities remain protected against evolving cyber threats.

Governance frameworks must also address incident response and remediation strategies for machine identity-related security breaches. Organizations must be prepared to respond quickly to incidents involving compromised machine identities, such as stolen API keys, unauthorized certificate issuance, or malicious use of service accounts. A well-defined incident response plan includes processes for identifying the root cause of the breach, revoking compromised identities, rotating credentials, and implementing additional security measures to prevent recurrence. By incorporating machine identity security into broader cybersecurity incident response strategies, organizations improve their ability to contain and mitigate threats effectively.

As machine identities continue to proliferate across enterprise environments, governance and compliance will remain critical for maintaining security and operational integrity. Organizations must establish structured governance frameworks that define policies, enforce security controls, and ensure compliance with regulatory requirements. By leveraging automation, continuous monitoring, risk management, and incident response capabilities, enterprises can secure their machine identities while minimizing security risks. Strengthening machine identity governance enables organizations to maintain trust, protect sensitive data, and reduce their exposure to cyber threats in an increasingly interconnected digital landscape.

Managing Machine Identities in Cloud Environments

Cloud computing has transformed the way enterprises deploy, manage, and secure their IT infrastructure. With the rapid adoption of cloud services, organizations now rely on virtual machines, containers, APIs, and serverless functions to run business-critical applications. Unlike traditional on-premises environments where machine identities were relatively static, cloud-based architectures introduce highly dynamic and ephemeral machine identities that require continuous management. As cloud workloads scale up and down based on demand, machine identities are constantly created, used, and decommissioned. Without proper oversight, these identities can become difficult to track, leading to security vulnerabilities, unauthorized access, and compliance risks.

Machine identities in cloud environments serve as the foundation for secure authentication, encryption, and access control between cloud services, applications, and external systems. These identities include digital certificates, API keys, SSH keys, cloud service accounts, and cryptographic tokens that machines use to authenticate and authorize interactions. Managing machine identities in the cloud requires a proactive approach that ensures all credentials are issued securely, rotated regularly, monitored for misuse, and revoked when no longer needed. Failure to implement strong machine identity management practices can lead to credential leaks, privilege escalation attacks, and data breaches.

Cloud platforms provide built-in identity and access management (IAM) solutions that help organizations secure machine identities. Cloud providers such as Amazon Web Services (AWS), Microsoft Azure, and Google Cloud Platform (GCP) offer IAM frameworks that allow administrators to define machine identity policies, assign roles, and enforce least privilege access. AWS IAM roles, Azure Managed Identities, and GCP Service Accounts enable cloud workloads to authenticate securely without requiring static credentials such as hardcoded passwords or API keys. By leveraging these cloud-native identity solutions, organizations can reduce the risk of credential exposure while maintaining centralized control over machine identities.

API security is a critical aspect of managing machine identities in cloud environments. Cloud applications rely heavily on APIs to communicate with other services, exchange data, and perform automated tasks. API keys, OAuth tokens, and mutual TLS (mTLS) certificates are commonly used to authenticate API interactions. Poor API key management, such as storing keys in plaintext configuration files or sharing them across multiple services, creates security risks. Attackers who gain access to exposed API keys can impersonate trusted services, bypass security controls, and exfiltrate sensitive data. To mitigate these risks, organizations should use secure API gateways, enforce key rotation policies, and implement token-based authentication mechanisms that limit the scope and duration of access.

The ephemeral nature of cloud resources further complicates machine identity management. Unlike traditional servers with long lifespans, cloud workloads such as containers, Kubernetes pods, and serverless functions often exist for only a few minutes or hours before being terminated. Each instance requires a unique machine identity for authentication and authorization, but managing thousands of short-lived credentials manually is impractical. Automated certificate management and just-in-time (JIT) credentials help address this challenge by provisioning temporary identities that automatically expire when no longer needed. Short-lived machine identities minimize the risk of credential theft, as attackers have a limited window of opportunity to exploit stolen credentials before they become invalid.

Key management plays an essential role in securing machine identities in the cloud. Cryptographic keys are used to encrypt data, sign transactions, and authenticate machine-to-machine interactions. Cloud providers offer key management services (KMS) that allow organizations to generate, store, and manage encryption keys securely. AWS Key Management Service (AWS KMS), Azure Key Vault, and Google Cloud KMS provide centralized control over encryption keys, enabling secure key distribution and automated rotation. Implementing strict access controls, logging key usage, and enforcing key expiration policies ensure that cryptographic assets remain protected from unauthorized access.

Certificate lifecycle management is another critical component of machine identity security in the cloud. Digital certificates issued by certificate authorities (CAs) enable encrypted communication between cloud workloads, applications, and external services. Expired or misconfigured certificates can cause authentication failures, disrupt services, and create security vulnerabilities. Automated certificate management platforms help organizations track certificate expiration dates, renew certificates before they expire, and revoke compromised credentials when necessary. By integrating certificate automation with cloud security policies, enterprises can maintain continuous trust in their machine identities while preventing service disruptions.

Monitoring and logging machine identity activity are essential for detecting anomalies and preventing security incidents. Cloud environments generate vast amounts of identity-related data, including authentication logs, access requests, and failed login attempts. Security teams must implement logging solutions that capture machine identity activity in real-time, allowing them to identify suspicious behavior such as unauthorized access attempts or unusual privilege escalations. Cloud-native security services, such as

AWS CloudTrail, Azure Monitor, and Google Cloud Logging, provide visibility into machine identity usage, enabling organizations to enforce security policies and respond to threats more effectively.

Compliance with regulatory frameworks is a key consideration when managing machine identities in the cloud. Industry regulations such as GDPR, HIPAA, PCI-DSS, and NIST require organizations to implement strong authentication, encryption, and access control measures for protecting sensitive data. Cloud environments introduce additional compliance challenges, as machine identities are distributed across multiple regions, services, and third-party integrations. Organizations must ensure that their cloud security policies align with regulatory requirements by enforcing identity governance frameworks, conducting regular audits, and maintaining detailed logs of identity activity. Demonstrating compliance with security standards helps enterprises avoid regulatory penalties while strengthening their overall security posture.

Automation is a crucial factor in managing machine identities at cloud scale. Manual identity management processes are time-consuming, error-prone, and unable to keep up with the rapid creation and decommissioning of cloud resources. Organizations must implement automated identity orchestration solutions that integrate with cloud IAM platforms, certificate management systems, and secrets management tools. By automating machine identity provisioning, renewal, and revocation, enterprises can reduce operational overhead, improve security consistency, and eliminate human errors that could lead to credential mismanagement.

The growing complexity of cloud architectures and the increasing number of machine identities require organizations to adopt a strategic approach to identity management. Security teams must establish policies that define how machine identities are issued, how long they remain valid, and what level of access they are granted. Machine identities should be continuously monitored for compliance with security policies, ensuring that unauthorized access is detected and mitigated before it leads to a security breach. Integrating cloud identity management with enterprise-wide security frameworks enables organizations to maintain control over machine identities while scaling their cloud operations securely.

Managing machine identities in cloud environments requires a combination of strong authentication mechanisms, automated identity lifecycle management, encryption key security, API protection, continuous monitoring, and compliance enforcement. Organizations that implement robust identity governance frameworks and leverage cloud-native security tools can minimize the risks associated with credential exposure, unauthorized access, and identity-based attacks. As cloud adoption continues to grow, securing machine identities will remain a top priority for enterprises seeking to protect their digital assets and maintain trust in their cloud infrastructure.

Protecting Machine Identities in Multi-Cloud Deployments

The rise of multi-cloud environments has introduced new challenges in managing and securing machine identities. Organizations are increasingly leveraging multiple cloud providers, such as Amazon Web Services (AWS), Microsoft Azure, and Google Cloud Platform (GCP), to distribute workloads, optimize costs, and improve resilience. While multi-cloud strategies offer numerous benefits, they also create complexities in managing authentication, encryption, and access control for machine identities across different cloud platforms. Each provider has its own identity and access management (IAM) framework, key management service, and security controls, making it difficult to maintain uniform policies and enforce consistent security standards. Without a comprehensive approach to protecting machine identities in multi-cloud deployments, organizations risk credential exposure, unauthorized access, and identity-based attacks that could compromise critical systems.

Machine identities in multi-cloud environments take various forms, including cloud service accounts, digital certificates, API keys, SSH keys, and cryptographic tokens. These identities authenticate workloads, enable secure communication between cloud services, and enforce access controls for applications and data storage. Managing these identities requires organizations to adopt a centralized governance framework that integrates with multiple cloud platforms, ensuring that security policies remain consistent and enforceable across different environments. Failure to establish a unified machine identity management strategy can lead to security gaps, increased attack surfaces, and difficulties in tracking identity activity across multiple providers.

A key challenge in multi-cloud machine identity security is the lack of standardization among cloud IAM solutions. AWS IAM roles, Azure Managed Identities, and GCP Service Accounts each function differently, requiring organizations to adapt their security strategies based on the specific capabilities of each provider. While these IAM solutions offer built-in identity management features, they operate independently, making it difficult to enforce cross-cloud policies. To address this challenge, organizations must implement a federated identity model that allows machine identities to be managed consistently across different cloud providers. Identity federation enables centralized authentication and access management, reducing complexity while improving visibility and control over machine identities.

Securing API keys and cloud credentials is a critical component of protecting machine identities in multi-cloud deployments. Many cloud-based applications rely on API keys to access cloud services, databases, and third-party integrations. However, improperly managed API keys pose a significant security risk, as they can be easily exposed, stolen, or misused by attackers. Organizations must implement strict policies for API key management, including secure storage in secrets management platforms, automatic key rotation, and access restrictions based on least privilege principles. Cloud providers offer secrets management services such as AWS Secrets Manager, Azure Key Vault, and Google Secret Manager, which allow organizations to store and manage sensitive credentials securely. By integrating these tools into their security workflows, enterprises can prevent unauthorized access to cloud resources while reducing the risk of credential leaks.

The ephemeral nature of cloud workloads further complicates machine identity protection in multi-cloud environments. Containers, serverless functions, and short-lived virtual machines are frequently deployed and terminated, generating temporary machine identities that must be secured throughout their lifecycle. Traditional identity management solutions struggle to keep up with these dynamic environments, requiring organizations to adopt automated certificate management and just-in-time (JIT) credential provisioning. Short-lived machine identities, combined with automatic expiration policies, ensure that credentials do not persist beyond their intended use, reducing the risk of compromise. Organizations that fail to implement automated identity lifecycle management may struggle to keep track of machine identities, leading to orphaned credentials that attackers can exploit.

Mutual Transport Layer Security (mTLS) is an effective security measure for protecting machine-to-machine communication in multi-cloud environments. By requiring both communicating machines to authenticate each other using digital certificates, mTLS ensures that only trusted identities can establish encrypted connections. Many cloud-native applications use mTLS to secure inter-service communication, particularly in microservices architectures where services constantly exchange data. Implementing mTLS across multi-cloud deployments requires organizations to maintain a centralized certificate authority (CA) or integrate with managed certificate services provided by cloud vendors. Automated certificate renewal and revocation policies help prevent service disruptions caused by expired certificates while maintaining a high level of security for machine identities.

Visibility and monitoring are crucial for detecting unauthorized access attempts and anomalies related to machine identities in multi-cloud environments. Security teams must implement centralized logging solutions that aggregate identity-related events across all cloud providers, ensuring that authentication failures, privilege escalations, and policy violations are detected in real-time. Cloud-native security tools such as AWS CloudTrail, Azure Monitor, and Google Cloud Logging provide detailed insights into machine identity activity, helping organizations identify potential threats and enforce security policies. Integrating these logs into a security information and event management (SIEM) system enables advanced threat detection and automated incident response.

Compliance with industry regulations and security standards is another critical aspect of protecting machine identities in multi-cloud deployments. Organizations operating in regulated industries must ensure that their identity management practices align with frameworks such as GDPR, HIPAA, PCI-DSS, and NIST. Multi-cloud environments introduce additional compliance challenges, as machine identities are distributed across different cloud providers, each with its own security policies and compliance requirements. To address these challenges, organizations must implement standardized machine identity governance frameworks that enforce encryption, access controls, and authentication policies consistently across all cloud platforms. Regular audits and compliance assessments help organizations identify security gaps and ensure that their machine identity management practices meet regulatory expectations.

Automation plays a crucial role in maintaining strong security controls for machine identities in multi-cloud environments. Manual identity management processes are insufficient to handle the scale and complexity of cloud deployments, leading to potential misconfigurations and security oversights. Organizations must leverage automation tools that integrate with multiple cloud providers, allowing them to streamline machine identity provisioning, certificate management, and policy enforcement. Identity orchestration platforms enable enterprises to centralize identity governance, enforce access controls dynamically, and detect anomalies in real-time. By automating machine identity security, organizations can reduce human error, improve operational efficiency, and maintain compliance with evolving security standards.

As organizations continue to expand their multi-cloud strategies, securing machine identities must remain a top priority to prevent unauthorized access, data breaches, and identity-based attacks. A robust security strategy for multi-cloud machine identity protection includes federated identity management, automated credential rotation, secure API key storage, mTLS enforcement, real-time monitoring, compliance alignment, and automated lifecycle management. By implementing these best practices, enterprises can establish a secure and resilient machine identity framework that protects their cloud workloads, maintains regulatory compliance, and mitigates emerging cybersecurity threats.

Best Practices for Securing IoT Device Identities

The rapid growth of the Internet of Things (IoT) has introduced a new set of security challenges, particularly in managing and securing IoT device identities. Unlike traditional IT assets, IoT devices operate in a wide range of environments, from industrial control systems and healthcare monitoring devices to smart home applications and connected vehicles. Each device must have a unique identity to authenticate itself, establish secure communications, and prevent unauthorized access. However, the sheer number of IoT devices, their diverse hardware and software ecosystems, and their often-limited computing capabilities make securing machine identities in IoT environments complex. Organizations must implement robust identity management strategies to mitigate security risks and ensure that IoT devices remain protected from cyber threats.

One of the fundamental practices for securing IoT device identities is implementing strong authentication mechanisms. Each IoT device must be uniquely identifiable, ensuring that only authorized devices can communicate within a network. Digital certificates issued by a trusted certificate authority (CA) provide a secure method for device authentication, enabling encrypted communications and preventing unauthorized access. Instead of relying on static credentials such as hardcoded passwords or pre-shared keys, IoT devices should use certificate-based authentication, where a public-private key pair verifies device legitimacy. This approach reduces the risk of credential compromise and eliminates common attack vectors such as password guessing and brute-force attacks.

Device identity provisioning must be performed securely to prevent unauthorized devices from being introduced into a network. When an IoT device is first deployed, it should undergo a secure onboarding process where its identity is registered and verified. Zero-touch provisioning (ZTP) automates this process by allowing IoT devices to enroll securely without requiring manual intervention. By using pre-configured identity credentials, devices can authenticate themselves to a central management system and receive security policies, certificates, and access controls. This eliminates the risk of human errors during manual provisioning and ensures that only trusted devices are added to the network.

Public key infrastructure (PKI) plays a crucial role in securing IoT device identities by providing a framework for issuing, managing, and revoking digital certificates. PKI-based authentication ensures that each IoT device has a cryptographically verifiable identity, preventing unauthorized devices from gaining access to sensitive networks. Organizations must establish scalable PKI infrastructures that support the high volume of IoT devices while enforcing automated certificate management. Regular certificate renewal and revocation policies help maintain the integrity of IoT device identities, ensuring that expired or compromised certificates cannot be exploited by attackers.

Strong encryption protocols must be enforced to protect data exchanged between IoT devices and backend systems. IoT devices often communicate sensitive information, such as telemetry data, sensor readings, and operational commands, which must be protected from eavesdropping and tampering. Transport Layer Security (TLS) provides end-to-end encryption, ensuring that data remains confidential during transmission. Mutual TLS (mTLS) strengthens security further by requiring both the IoT device and the receiving system to authenticate each other using digital certificates. Organizations must ensure that IoT devices support modern encryption standards and disable outdated or weak cryptographic algorithms to prevent exploits.

Access control policies should be applied to restrict IoT device privileges and prevent unauthorized actions. IoT devices should operate under the principle of least privilege, meaning they should only have the minimum access necessary to perform their intended functions. Role-based access control (RBAC) and attribute-based access control (ABAC) frameworks help define access policies that regulate device interactions with other systems. If an IoT device is only required to send sensor data, it should not have permissions to modify configurations or access unrelated network resources. Implementing strict access control policies reduces the attack surface and minimizes the impact of potential security breaches.

IoT devices must be continuously monitored to detect suspicious activity and prevent identity compromise. Organizations should implement real-time logging and anomaly detection systems that track authentication attempts, failed login attempts, and unexpected behavioral changes. Security information and event management (SIEM) platforms provide visibility into IoT device activity, allowing security teams to detect anomalies such as a device attempting to communicate with unauthorized systems or transmitting unexpected data. Automated alerts and response mechanisms help organizations react quickly to potential security threats, mitigating risks before they escalate into full-scale breaches.

Regular software and firmware updates are essential to maintaining IoT device security. Many IoT devices run on embedded systems that require periodic updates to patch vulnerabilities and improve security features. Devices should support secure firmware updates that are cryptographically signed and verified before installation, preventing unauthorized code modifications. Over-the-air (OTA) update mechanisms enable organizations to remotely update IoT devices, ensuring that security patches are deployed efficiently across large-scale IoT deployments. Devices that cannot receive updates due to hardware limitations or vendor restrictions should be carefully monitored for vulnerabilities and phased out when necessary.

Supply chain security is a critical consideration for securing IoT device identities. Organizations must ensure that devices are manufactured, configured, and distributed securely, preventing tampering and unauthorized modifications before deployment. Secure boot mechanisms verify the integrity of the device firmware at startup, ensuring that only trusted software is executed. Hardware security modules (HSMs) and trusted platform modules (TPMs) provide additional layers of protection by securely storing cryptographic keys and preventing unauthorized access. Organizations must conduct security assessments of their IoT supply chains to identify potential risks and enforce strict security controls throughout the device lifecycle.

Automated identity lifecycle management helps organizations maintain control over IoT device identities as devices are added, used, and eventually decommissioned. When an IoT device reaches the end of its lifecycle, its identity credentials must be revoked to prevent unauthorized access. If device identities are not properly decommissioned, attackers may exploit lingering credentials to impersonate legitimate devices and gain access to enterprise networks. Automated identity revocation policies ensure that unused device identities are removed from authentication systems, reducing security risks and preventing unauthorized access after a device is retired.

Scalability is a key challenge in securing IoT device identities, particularly in environments with thousands or millions of connected devices. Traditional identity management approaches struggle to handle the sheer volume of IoT machine identities, requiring organizations to adopt scalable identity management solutions. Cloud-based identity platforms provide centralized visibility and policy enforcement, enabling organizations to manage IoT device identities at scale. By leveraging automation, artificial intelligence, and machine learning, enterprises can detect anomalies, enforce security policies, and maintain real-time compliance across large-scale IoT deployments.

As IoT adoption continues to expand across industries, securing device identities is critical to protecting enterprise networks, sensitive data, and connected ecosystems. Organizations must implement a combination of strong authentication, encryption, access control, monitoring, and automated lifecycle management to safeguard IoT device identities. By enforcing best practices, continuously assessing security risks, and adopting scalable identity management solutions, enterprises can mitigate threats, reduce attack surfaces, and ensure that their IoT deployments remain secure in an increasingly connected world.

DevOps and Machine Identity Security

The adoption of DevOps practices has revolutionized software development and IT operations, enabling organizations to accelerate application delivery, automate infrastructure provisioning, and improve overall efficiency. However, the speed and automation that DevOps introduces also create new security challenges, particularly in managing machine identities. In a DevOps-driven environment, machine identities—including digital certificates, API keys, SSH keys, and cryptographic tokens—play a critical role in authenticating workloads, securing communication between services, and enforcing access control policies. Without proper security measures, machine identities can become an easy target for cybercriminals, leading to unauthorized access, privilege escalation, and data breaches.

Machine identity security in DevOps is especially challenging due to the highly dynamic nature of development pipelines. Unlike traditional IT environments where machines and applications have relatively static identities, DevOps relies on ephemeral workloads, containers, and serverless functions that are frequently created and destroyed. Each instance requires a unique machine identity to authenticate itself, but managing a vast number of short-lived identities manually is impractical. Security teams must implement automated machine identity management solutions that integrate seamlessly with DevOps workflows, ensuring that identities are issued, rotated, and revoked in real time without disrupting development velocity.

One of the key aspects of securing machine identities in DevOps is automating the issuance and management of digital certificates. In continuous integration and continuous deployment (CI/CD) pipelines, applications and services communicate through APIs, microservices, and cloud-native architectures that require encrypted communication. Digital certificates based on public key infrastructure (PKI) provide a secure method for machine authentication, but manually managing these certificates in a fast-paced DevOps environment is not feasible. Organizations must integrate automated certificate management solutions that dynamically issue and renew certificates, preventing outages caused by expired credentials and reducing the risk of certificate misconfigurations.

Secrets management is another crucial component of machine identity security in DevOps. API keys, SSH credentials, and authentication tokens are frequently used to enable automated processes and connect various components of an application. If these credentials are not properly secured, they can be exposed in source code repositories, configuration files, or logging systems, making them vulnerable to theft and misuse. DevOps teams should use secrets management tools such as HashiCorp Vault, AWS Secrets Manager, Azure Key Vault, or Google Secret Manager to store and protect machine identity credentials. Implementing role-based access controls (RBAC) and just-in-time access mechanisms ensures that secrets are only accessible to authorized services and personnel, minimizing the risk of credential leaks.

Machine identity rotation and revocation policies are essential in preventing long-term credential exposure. Static credentials that persist for extended periods become an attractive target for attackers, as they provide a reliable entry point into an organization's infrastructure. DevOps teams must enforce automated key rotation policies that periodically generate new cryptographic credentials, reducing the window of opportunity for malicious actors to exploit stolen identities. Additionally, when a service, container, or virtual machine is decommissioned, its associated identities must be revoked to prevent unauthorized access. Continuous monitoring of identity usage ensures that expired or orphaned credentials do not remain active, reducing the risk of identity sprawl.

Mutual TLS (mTLS) provides an additional layer of security for machine-to-machine authentication in DevOps environments. In microservices architectures, services must verify each other's identities before exchanging data, preventing unauthorized services from injecting malicious payloads. mTLS ensures that both the client and server authenticate each other using digital certificates, establishing a trusted communication channel. By enforcing mTLS across CI/CD pipelines and cloud-native deployments, organizations can prevent man-in-the-middle attacks and unauthorized service access. Automated certificate renewal mechanisms ensure that mTLS authentication remains uninterrupted, even as services scale dynamically.

Infrastructure as Code (IaC) introduces new machine identity security considerations, as it allows DevOps teams to define and provision infrastructure programmatically. Tools like Terraform, Ansible, and Kubernetes use configuration files to deploy resources, often requiring authentication credentials to interact with cloud services and APIs. If these credentials are hardcoded into configuration files or scripts, they can be exposed in code repositories and version control systems, leading to security vulnerabilities. DevOps teams must enforce best practices such as using environment variables, secrets managers, and IAM roles to securely handle machine identities within IaC frameworks. Implementing automated security scans for infrastructure code helps detect misconfigured credentials before they become a security risk.

Zero Trust security principles align closely with DevOps machine identity security by enforcing continuous verification of all entities, regardless of their location within the network. In a Zero Trust model, no machine or service is implicitly trusted, and access is granted based on strict identity validation and real-time risk assessments. Implementing Zero Trust in DevOps environments requires enforcing strong authentication, limiting machine identity privileges, and continuously monitoring service interactions for anomalous behavior. Integrating identity-aware proxies and policy-based access controls ensures that only verified machines and services can interact within the DevOps ecosystem.

Logging and monitoring machine identity activity are critical for detecting unauthorized access attempts and security threats. DevOps environments generate extensive logs related to authentication events, identity usage, and access requests. Security teams must aggregate these logs into centralized security information and event management (SIEM) systems to analyze identity behaviors and detect anomalies. Advanced analytics, machine learning-based threat detection, and automated response mechanisms help identify compromised machine identities before they can be exploited. By maintaining comprehensive visibility into machine identity usage, organizations can quickly respond to security incidents and enforce compliance with regulatory requirements.

Regulatory compliance is another key consideration when securing machine identities in DevOps. Organizations operating in industries such as finance, healthcare, and government must adhere to strict security standards, including GDPR, HIPAA, PCI-DSS, and NIST guidelines. These regulations mandate strong authentication, encryption, and identity governance practices to protect sensitive data and prevent unauthorized access. DevOps teams must integrate compliance controls into their CI/CD workflows, ensuring that all machine identities meet regulatory requirements. Automating compliance reporting and conducting regular security audits help organizations demonstrate adherence to industry standards while mitigating potential risks.

Security and agility must coexist in DevOps environments, requiring organizations to implement security measures that do not hinder development speed. By integrating automated identity management solutions, enforcing strict access controls, and adopting Zero Trust security models, DevOps teams can secure machine identities while maintaining the efficiency of their workflows. Machine identity security should be treated as a foundational component of DevOps pipelines, embedded into development processes rather than applied as a separate layer of security. Organizations that prioritize machine identity protection in DevOps can prevent identity-related breaches, reduce attack surfaces, and ensure the integrity of their cloud-native applications and automated workflows.

Machine Identity Management in CI/CD Pipelines

Continuous Integration and Continuous Deployment (CI/CD) pipelines have become a fundamental part of modern software development, allowing organizations to automate the building, testing, and deployment of applications. These pipelines enable rapid development cycles, ensuring that software updates can be delivered quickly and efficiently. However, the automation and interconnected nature of CI/CD environments introduce significant security challenges, particularly in managing machine identities. Every component in a CI/CD pipeline—including build servers, containers, cloud environments, source code repositories, and deployment tools—relies on machine identities to authenticate, authorize, and securely communicate with other services. If machine identities are not properly managed, they can become an entry point for attackers to infiltrate the pipeline, compromise source code, and manipulate production environments.

Machine identities in CI/CD pipelines take multiple forms, including API keys, digital certificates, SSH keys, authentication tokens, and service accounts. These identities are used to grant automated processes access to code repositories, cloud infrastructure, testing environments, and production systems. Unlike human identities, which are managed through user authentication and role-based access controls, machine identities must be dynamically created, used, and revoked in real-time as the pipeline executes different stages of the software development lifecycle. Without proper lifecycle management, machine identities can be exposed in logs, hardcoded into scripts, or left active beyond their intended use, creating security vulnerabilities that attackers can exploit.

One of the most significant risks in CI/CD pipelines is the exposure of machine identity credentials in source code repositories. Developers often use API keys, authentication tokens, and SSH credentials to enable automated scripts and deployment processes. If these credentials are hardcoded into source code and pushed to a version control system, they become accessible to anyone with access to the repository. Publicly exposed credentials can be exploited by attackers to gain unauthorized access to critical infrastructure. Organizations must enforce strict security policies that prevent hardcoded secrets in source code by integrating secret scanning tools that detect and remove exposed credentials before they are committed.

Secrets management plays a crucial role in securing machine identities in CI/CD pipelines. Instead of storing credentials in configuration files or environment variables, organizations should use dedicated secrets management solutions such as HashiCorp Vault, AWS Secrets Manager, Azure Key Vault, or Google Secret Manager. These tools provide secure storage and access control mechanisms for API keys, encryption keys, and authentication tokens. Secrets should be dynamically injected into CI/CD pipelines only when needed and automatically revoked after use to minimize the risk of credential theft. Implementing just-in-time (JIT) credential provisioning further enhances security by generating temporary machine identities that expire after a defined period.

Automating certificate management is another critical aspect of securing machine identities in CI/CD pipelines. Digital certificates enable encrypted communication between pipeline components, cloud services, and deployed applications. However, managing these certificates manually is impractical, as they require frequent renewal and revocation. Organizations should integrate automated certificate management solutions that issue and rotate certificates dynamically, ensuring that machine identities remain up to date. Public Key Infrastructure (PKI) can be leveraged to establish trust between pipeline components, enforcing strong authentication and encryption standards throughout the software development lifecycle.

Zero Trust principles should be applied to machine identity management in CI/CD pipelines, ensuring that no entity—whether human or machine—is automatically trusted. Every machine identity must authenticate itself before accessing a resource, and access should be granted based on least privilege principles. Role-based access control (RBAC) and attribute-based access control (ABAC) frameworks help define fine-grained permissions for machine identities, ensuring that automated processes can only interact with specific services and data necessary for their function. By enforcing strong access controls, organizations can minimize the impact of a compromised machine identity and prevent privilege escalation attacks.

Logging and monitoring machine identity activity in CI/CD pipelines are essential for detecting anomalies and potential security threats. Every authentication attempt, access request, and identity-based action should be logged and analyzed for suspicious behavior. Security teams should integrate pipeline logs with security information and event management (SIEM) platforms to identify unauthorized access attempts, privilege escalation attempts, and unusual API activity. Automated anomaly detection using machine learning can help flag potential security incidents in real-time, allowing for immediate remediation before attackers can exploit vulnerabilities.

Pipeline security scanning should be an integral part of machine identity management in CI/CD workflows. Static analysis security testing (SAST) and dynamic analysis security testing (DAST) tools can detect vulnerabilities in code that may expose machine identities or create security weaknesses. Infrastructure as Code (IaC) scanning ensures that misconfigurations related to machine identity permissions, authentication settings, and access controls are identified before deployment. Regular security scans provide continuous assurance that machine identities are properly managed and do not introduce risks into the development process.

DevOps teams must establish clear governance policies for machine identity management in CI/CD environments. Policies should define how machine identities are issued, how long they remain active, and how they are revoked after use. Identity lifecycle management must be automated to ensure that expired or unused credentials are promptly deactivated, reducing the risk of unauthorized access. Regular audits of CI/CD pipelines help identify compliance gaps and enforce security best practices. Organizations operating in regulated industries must ensure that their machine identity management practices align with frameworks such as GDPR, HIPAA, PCI-DSS, and NIST, which mandate strict access control and encryption requirements.

Cloud-native security solutions provide additional layers of protection for machine identities in CI/CD pipelines. Cloud service providers offer identity and access management (IAM) capabilities that allow organizations to enforce security policies for machine identities at scale. AWS IAM roles, Azure Managed Identities, and Google Cloud Service Accounts enable secure authentication without exposing static credentials. By integrating CI/CD pipelines with cloud IAM solutions, organizations can enforce dynamic identity management policies that adapt to evolving security requirements.

Security automation is key to maintaining the integrity of machine identities in CI/CD environments. Organizations must implement automated policy enforcement mechanisms that detect security misconfigurations, enforce identity rotation policies, and revoke compromised credentials in real-time. Identity orchestration solutions streamline machine identity governance, ensuring that security controls are consistently applied across different pipeline stages. By embedding security into DevOps workflows from the beginning, organizations can build secure-by-design CI/CD pipelines that minimize identity-related risks and prevent unauthorized access to critical infrastructure.

As software development continues to evolve towards rapid automation and cloud-native architectures, the security of machine identities in CI/CD pipelines must be a top priority. Attackers actively target mismanaged credentials, exposed secrets, and weak identity controls to infiltrate DevOps environments. By implementing robust identity lifecycle management, enforcing least privilege access, securing secrets, and integrating continuous monitoring, organizations can protect their CI/CD pipelines from identity-based threats. A proactive approach to machine identity security ensures that automated processes remain secure, reliable, and resistant to cyber threats, enabling organizations to maintain trust in their software delivery pipelines.

Protecting Containers and Kubernetes Machine Identities

Containers and Kubernetes have transformed modern application development by enabling organizations to deploy, scale, and manage applications more efficiently. Unlike traditional virtual machines, containers are lightweight, portable, and ephemeral, making them ideal for cloud-native environments. However, the dynamic nature of containers also introduces security challenges, particularly in managing machine identities. Each container, Kubernetes pod, and microservice requires an identity to authenticate itself, communicate securely, and access resources. Without proper security measures, attackers can exploit mismanaged machine identities to gain unauthorized access, compromise workloads, and move laterally within a cluster. Protecting container and Kubernetes machine identities is essential for maintaining a secure cloud-native ecosystem.

Machine identities in Kubernetes take various forms, including service accounts, API keys, digital certificates, and cryptographic tokens. These identities are used to authenticate workloads, enforce access controls, and establish secure communication between services. Kubernetes provides built-in identity mechanisms through service accounts, which allow pods to authenticate with the Kubernetes API and other external services. However, if not properly managed, service accounts can be misconfigured, overprivileged, or exposed to unauthorized entities, leading to security vulnerabilities.

Organizations must enforce strict policies that limit service account privileges, ensuring that workloads operate under the principle of least privilege and cannot access resources beyond their intended scope.

Securing Kubernetes service accounts requires implementing role-based access control (RBAC) to define granular permissions for machine identities. By default, Kubernetes assigns a default service account to each pod, which may have excessive permissions if not properly restricted. Organizations should create custom service accounts with specific roles and bindings that limit access to only necessary resources. RBAC policies should be continuously reviewed and updated to prevent privilege escalation and unauthorized access. Implementing audit logs for service account activity helps detect suspicious behavior, such as unexpected API calls or unauthorized service-to-service communication.

API authentication and authorization play a critical role in protecting Kubernetes machine identities. The Kubernetes API server is the central component that manages cluster operations, and any compromised identity with API access can lead to full cluster takeover. Organizations must enforce strong authentication mechanisms such as client certificates, OpenID Connect (OIDC), or Kubernetes authentication plugins to ensure that only trusted entities can interact with the API server. Mutual TLS (mTLS) can further enhance security by requiring both client and server authentication before establishing communication. Enforcing API rate limiting and monitoring API access logs help prevent brute-force attacks and unauthorized API requests.

Secrets management is another key aspect of securing Kubernetes machine identities. Containers often require sensitive credentials such as database passwords, API tokens, and encryption keys to function properly. Storing these secrets in plaintext within configuration files or environment variables creates significant security risks, as attackers can extract them from compromised containers. Kubernetes provides a built-in secrets management system that allows organizations to securely store and distribute credentials to pods. However, Kubernetes secrets are stored in etcd by default and must be encrypted at rest to prevent unauthorized access. Using external secrets management solutions such as HashiCorp Vault, AWS Secrets Manager, or Azure

Key Vault can provide additional layers of protection, ensuring that secrets are securely managed and rotated periodically.

Container runtime security is essential for protecting machine identities within Kubernetes environments. Attackers can exploit vulnerabilities in containerized applications to gain access to running containers, steal credentials, or execute malicious code. Implementing runtime security policies using tools such as Kubernetes Pod Security Standards (PSS) and Open Policy Agent (OPA) helps enforce security best practices, such as preventing privilege escalation, restricting container capabilities, and blocking unauthorized system calls. Runtime monitoring solutions such as Falco can detect anomalous behavior in containers, alerting security teams to potential identity compromise or unauthorized access attempts.

Network security controls play a vital role in securing Kubernetes machine identities and preventing unauthorized communication between workloads. Kubernetes network policies allow administrators to define rules that restrict traffic between pods based on identity, namespace, and labels. By implementing zero trust network segmentation, organizations can ensure that only authorized services can communicate with each other, reducing the risk of lateral movement attacks. Using a service mesh such as Istio or Linkerd can further enhance security by providing mTLS encryption, traffic monitoring, and identity-based access control for microservices. Service meshes help establish secure communication channels between containers while preventing unauthorized access to sensitive data.

Automating certificate management is critical for ensuring the integrity of Kubernetes machine identities. Kubernetes uses certificates for securing API communication, encrypting etcd storage, and authenticating services within a cluster. However, managing certificates manually is not scalable in dynamic container environments. Organizations should leverage automated certificate management solutions such as cert-manager to issue, renew, and revoke certificates automatically. Integrating certificate lifecycle management with Kubernetes ensures that machine identities remain valid and secure throughout their usage. Expired or misconfigured certificates can lead to authentication failures and security gaps, making automation a crucial component of Kubernetes identity security.

Logging and monitoring Kubernetes machine identity activity provide visibility into potential security threats. Kubernetes audit logs capture events related to authentication, authorization, and service account usage, allowing security teams to track anomalous behavior. Aggregating logs with centralized security information and event management (SIEM) systems helps detect identity-based attacks, such as unauthorized API requests, unexpected privilege escalations, or compromised service accounts. Using anomaly detection and behavioral analytics can enhance threat detection, allowing organizations to respond proactively to identity-related security incidents.

Compliance and regulatory considerations must be addressed when managing Kubernetes machine identities, particularly in industries subject to strict security requirements. Frameworks such as GDPR, HIPAA, PCI-DSS, and NIST require organizations to implement strong authentication, encryption, and access control measures to protect sensitive data. Kubernetes security policies must align with these compliance standards, ensuring that machine identities adhere to best practices for identity governance. Regular security audits, policy enforcement, and risk assessments help maintain compliance while improving overall security posture.

As containerized applications and Kubernetes adoption continue to grow, organizations must prioritize the security of machine identities to prevent unauthorized access, identity theft, and service disruptions. By enforcing strong authentication mechanisms, securing API access, implementing RBAC, encrypting secrets, monitoring network activity, and automating certificate management, enterprises can establish a robust security framework for protecting Kubernetes machine identities. A proactive approach to security ensures that containerized workloads remain protected against evolving threats, enabling organizations to deploy applications with confidence while maintaining the integrity of their cloud-native infrastructure.

Securing APIs and Service-to-Service Communications

APIs serve as the backbone of modern digital infrastructure, enabling applications, cloud services, and microservices to interact seamlessly. As organizations increasingly adopt cloud-native architectures and distributed systems, the security of APIs and service-to-service communications becomes a critical concern. APIs expose sensitive data, business logic, and functionality to external and internal consumers, making them a prime target for cyberattacks. Unauthorized access, API abuse, and identity spoofing can lead to data breaches, service disruptions, and security vulnerabilities. Implementing strong security measures for APIs and machine identities is essential to protect enterprise applications, ensure compliance, and mitigate evolving cyber threats.

Machine identities play a crucial role in securing API interactions, as automated services must authenticate and authorize each other before exchanging data. Unlike human authentication, which relies on usernames, passwords, and multi-factor authentication, machine authentication uses digital certificates, API keys, OAuth tokens, and cryptographic signatures to establish trust between services. Proper management of machine identities ensures that only authorized systems can invoke APIs, preventing unauthorized access and reducing the risk of API-related attacks. Organizations must enforce identity governance policies that regulate how machine identities are issued, stored, rotated, and revoked to maintain secure API communications.

Authentication is the first layer of API security, ensuring that only verified entities can access API endpoints. API authentication methods vary based on security requirements, with OAuth 2.0, JSON Web Tokens (JWT), API keys, and mutual TLS (mTLS) being the most commonly used mechanisms. OAuth 2.0 provides a secure delegation-based authentication framework, allowing applications to obtain temporary access tokens without exposing sensitive credentials. JWTs enhance security by enabling stateless authentication, where signed tokens verify a machine's identity and authorization claims. Mutual TLS strengthens authentication by requiring both client and server certificates, ensuring encrypted and trusted communication between

APIs. Implementing strong authentication protocols minimizes the risk of credential theft, unauthorized API access, and identity impersonation.

Authorization mechanisms define what actions an authenticated machine identity can perform within an API ecosystem. Role-based access control (RBAC) and attribute-based access control (ABAC) frameworks help enforce least privilege access, ensuring that machine identities can only interact with specific API endpoints based on predefined permissions. RBAC assigns roles to machine identities, restricting access based on assigned privileges, while ABAC evaluates contextual attributes such as device type, location, and security posture before granting access. Implementing fine-grained authorization policies prevents overprivileged access, mitigating the risk of API abuse and unauthorized data exposure.

API security also requires implementing encryption for data in transit and at rest. Transport Layer Security (TLS) ensures that API communications remain encrypted, protecting sensitive data from interception and man-in-the-middle attacks. Mutual TLS (mTLS) enhances security by enforcing bidirectional authentication, verifying both the client and server identities before initiating an encrypted connection. Organizations must enforce strong TLS configurations, disable outdated encryption protocols, and regularly rotate certificates to maintain secure API communication channels. Encrypting API responses, sensitive payloads, and stored data further enhances protection against unauthorized access and data breaches.

Rate limiting and throttling mechanisms protect APIs from abuse and denial-of-service (DoS) attacks. Without proper rate limits, malicious actors can overwhelm API endpoints with excessive requests, leading to service degradation and potential outages. API gateways enforce request rate limits, restricting the number of API calls a machine identity can make within a specific time frame. Throttling further prevents API misuse by dynamically adjusting request limits based on real-time usage patterns. By implementing rate limiting and throttling policies, organizations can prevent API overload, reduce the risk of automated attacks, and maintain service availability.

API logging and monitoring provide essential visibility into service-to-service interactions, helping detect security threats and anomalies. Logging API access requests, authentication attempts, and error responses allows security teams to track machine identity activity and identify suspicious behavior. Security Information and Event Management (SIEM) systems aggregate API logs, enabling advanced threat detection, anomaly analysis, and automated response capabilities. Implementing real-time API monitoring helps organizations detect API abuse, unauthorized access attempts, and data exfiltration, allowing for proactive security measures to be taken before incidents escalate.

API security testing is a critical practice to identify vulnerabilities and misconfigurations before they can be exploited. Static API security testing (SAST) analyzes API code and configurations for security flaws, while dynamic API security testing (DAST) simulates real-world attacks to uncover runtime vulnerabilities. Penetration testing further evaluates API resilience against exploitation attempts, ensuring that authentication, authorization, and encryption mechanisms function as intended. Regular API security assessments help organizations uncover security gaps, remediate vulnerabilities, and strengthen API defenses against evolving threats.

API gateways and service meshes enhance security by providing centralized control over API traffic, authentication, and policy enforcement. API gateways act as a security layer that manages API requests, implements rate limits, and enforces authentication policies before routing requests to backend services. Service meshes, such as Istio and Linkerd, provide fine-grained security controls for microservices, enabling mutual TLS encryption, traffic monitoring, and access control enforcement at the service level. Integrating API gateways and service meshes into an API security strategy ensures consistent policy enforcement, reduces attack surfaces, and enhances visibility into API interactions.

Compliance and regulatory requirements mandate stringent API security practices to protect sensitive data and maintain regulatory compliance. Regulations such as GDPR, HIPAA, PCI-DSS, and NIST require organizations to implement authentication, encryption, and access control measures to secure API communications. API security policies must align with compliance frameworks, ensuring that machine identities, authentication methods, and data encryption practices adhere to regulatory standards. Conducting regular compliance audits and security assessments helps organizations demonstrate adherence to security best practices while mitigating legal and financial risks associated with non-compliance.

Automating API security helps organizations enforce consistent security policies across distributed environments. Manual API identity management introduces human errors, security gaps, and operational inefficiencies. Automated identity governance solutions streamline API authentication, access control, and credential lifecycle management, reducing the risk of misconfigured API permissions. Identity orchestration platforms integrate with API gateways, cloud IAM services, and security monitoring tools to enforce machine identity policies dynamically. By automating API security, organizations can enhance protection, improve scalability, and maintain security resilience across modern cloud-native architectures.

As APIs continue to serve as a critical foundation for digital transformation, securing API interactions and service-to-service communications must be a top priority. Attackers actively target APIs to exploit vulnerabilities, gain unauthorized access, and disrupt business operations. Implementing strong authentication, fine-grained authorization, encryption, rate limiting, logging, and automated security controls ensures that API communications remain protected against evolving threats. By adopting a comprehensive API security strategy, organizations can safeguard their digital ecosystems, prevent API abuse, and maintain the trust and reliability of their services.

Automation of Machine Identity Management

Machine identity management has become a critical aspect of enterprise security as organizations increasingly rely on automated systems, cloud environments, and interconnected applications. Every machine, including cloud workloads, APIs, microservices, IoT devices, and containers, requires authentication and authorization to ensure secure communication and prevent unauthorized access. The scale at which machine identities are generated, used, and revoked makes manual identity management impractical. Without automation, organizations risk security gaps, credential sprawl, and misconfigurations that could lead to data breaches, system outages, and compliance violations. Automating machine identity management is essential for maintaining security, reducing operational overhead, and ensuring consistent policy enforcement across distributed environments.

The automation of machine identity management begins with the issuance and provisioning of machine identities. When a new system, application, or service is deployed, it requires authentication credentials such as digital certificates, API keys, SSH keys, or cryptographic tokens. Automating the identity issuance process ensures that each machine receives a unique and properly configured identity without requiring manual intervention. Public Key Infrastructure (PKI) plays a crucial role in this process by issuing digital certificates that authenticate machines. Certificate automation platforms such as cert-manager, AWS Certificate Manager, and Let's Encrypt enable organizations to dynamically provision certificates, ensuring that all machine identities follow standardized security policies.

Once machine identities are issued, automated lifecycle management ensures that they remain valid, secure, and up to date. Unlike human identities, which are relatively stable, machine identities frequently change due to dynamic cloud environments, containerized workloads, and DevOps-driven automation. Automated certificate renewal prevents expired credentials from causing authentication failures and service disruptions. Implementing just-in-time (JIT) identity provisioning further enhances security by issuing temporary credentials that expire automatically after use. By automating lifecycle management, organizations can eliminate the risks associated with stale, orphaned, or misconfigured machine identities.

Credential rotation is another essential aspect of machine identity automation. Static credentials, such as hardcoded API keys, encryption keys, and service account tokens, are a major security risk. If a credential is compromised, an attacker can use it indefinitely unless it is revoked or rotated. Automated key rotation policies enforce periodic credential updates, ensuring that compromised credentials are rendered useless before they can be exploited. Identity orchestration platforms integrate with cloud services, secrets management solutions, and identity and access management (IAM) frameworks to enforce automatic key rotation without disrupting business operations.

Automated identity governance provides continuous visibility into machine identity usage, ensuring that security policies are consistently applied. Organizations must track which machines are using specific credentials, how they are being accessed, and whether they comply with security best practices. Machine identity governance platforms enforce policy-based controls that define identity issuance criteria, expiration timelines, and access restrictions. Logging and monitoring identity usage across cloud and on-premises environments allow security teams to detect anomalies, unauthorized access attempts, and identity misuse. By leveraging automation, organizations can eliminate blind spots and enforce compliance with regulatory frameworks such as GDPR, HIPAA, PCI-DSS, and NIST.

Machine-to-machine authentication must be continuously monitored and secured through automated mechanisms. Modern cloud environments rely on service-to-service interactions, where applications communicate using machine identities. Mutual Transport Layer Security (mTLS) automates authentication by requiring both the client and server to verify each other's identity before exchanging data. Automated certificate management solutions ensure that mTLS certificates are issued, renewed, and revoked dynamically, reducing the risk of authentication failures caused by expired credentials. Integrating automated authentication mechanisms with API gateways and service meshes enhances security by enforcing identity-based access control for all machine-to-machine interactions.

Secrets management automation is critical for protecting sensitive machine credentials. Storing credentials in plaintext files, environment variables, or application code creates a significant security risk, as attackers can easily extract and exploit them. Secrets management tools such as HashiCorp Vault, AWS Secrets Manager, Azure Key Vault, and Google Secret Manager provide automated storage, retrieval, and rotation of machine credentials. Role-based access control (RBAC) and attribute-based access control (ABAC) frameworks enforce access restrictions, ensuring that only authorized machines can retrieve secrets. Automating secrets management eliminates human error, reduces credential exposure, and strengthens security posture.

The integration of machine identity automation with DevOps and CI/CD pipelines ensures that security is embedded into the software development lifecycle. In DevOps environments, machines frequently spin up and down as part of automated deployment workflows. Each build process, container instance, and Kubernetes pod requires an identity to interact with other services securely. Automating identity issuance and enforcement within CI/CD pipelines prevents misconfigurations that could expose credentials to unauthorized users. Identity orchestration tools integrate with container orchestration platforms, ensuring that machine identities are provisioned dynamically as workloads scale. By embedding security automation into DevOps processes, organizations can enforce consistent identity policies while maintaining agility.

Machine identity risk detection and response benefit from automation by enabling real-time security monitoring and remediation. Security information and event management (SIEM) systems aggregate machine identity logs, providing insights into authentication failures, unexpected credential usage, and potential threats. Automated anomaly detection powered by machine learning helps identify deviations from normal identity behavior, triggering alerts or automated responses. For example, if a machine identity suddenly accesses resources outside its normal scope, an automated response system can revoke credentials, block access, or trigger further investigation. By integrating automated threat detection with identity management, organizations can respond to security incidents in real time, reducing the likelihood of successful attacks.

Scalability is a major advantage of automating machine identity management, allowing organizations to handle thousands or millions of identities without increasing administrative overhead. As businesses expand their cloud footprint, IoT deployments, and microservices architectures, the number of machine identities continues to grow. Manual identity management processes are not sustainable in highly dynamic environments, requiring enterprises to adopt automated identity orchestration solutions. Cloud-native security frameworks provide identity lifecycle automation that scales with business needs, ensuring that machine identities remain secure even as infrastructure evolves.

Regulatory compliance and audit readiness are strengthened through automation, as identity governance frameworks generate real-time compliance reports and enforce standardized security policies. Organizations operating in regulated industries must demonstrate that they manage machine identities according to security best practices. Automated audit trails provide detailed records of identity issuance, renewal, access attempts, and revocations, simplifying compliance reporting. Continuous compliance monitoring ensures that organizations remain aligned with regulatory requirements, reducing the risk of compliance violations and associated penalties.

As the digital landscape evolves, organizations must prioritize the automation of machine identity management to protect against credential-based attacks, unauthorized access, and identity misconfigurations. Automating identity issuance, lifecycle management, rotation, authentication, governance, and risk detection enhances security while reducing operational complexity. By integrating automated identity management solutions with cloud security frameworks, DevOps workflows, and compliance monitoring tools, organizations can ensure that their machine identities remain protected, scalable, and resilient in an increasingly interconnected world.

Artificial Intelligence and Machine Identity Threats

The rise of artificial intelligence has transformed cybersecurity, introducing both defensive capabilities and new threats to machine identity security. AI-powered tools can enhance security posture by detecting anomalies, automating threat responses, and strengthening authentication processes. However, the same advancements in AI have also enabled cybercriminals to launch more sophisticated attacks on machine identities. Malicious actors leverage AI-driven techniques to bypass authentication mechanisms, exploit identity vulnerabilities, and manipulate automated systems at an unprecedented scale. Organizations must understand how AI contributes to emerging machine identity threats and develop countermeasures to protect their digital ecosystems.

One of the most concerning AI-driven threats to machine identities is the ability to automate credential theft and identity compromise. Attackers use AI-powered bots to scan code repositories, cloud storage, and publicly accessible systems for exposed API keys, digital certificates, and cryptographic credentials. These bots operate at high speed, identifying vulnerabilities that human attackers might overlook. AI-driven password cracking algorithms can break weak or poorly managed credentials within seconds, enabling attackers to hijack machine identities and impersonate legitimate systems. Organizations must implement strict security policies, including automated secret scanning, robust authentication methods, and frequent credential rotation, to prevent AI-assisted credential theft.

AI also enables highly advanced phishing and social engineering attacks that target machine identities. Traditional phishing campaigns rely on human deception, but AI-powered phishing tools can generate personalized messages, clone legitimate login pages, and bypass security filters with greater accuracy. Attackers use AI to craft spear-phishing emails that manipulate DevOps teams into revealing API credentials, SSH keys, or certificate access. AI-driven deepfake technologies further complicate security by creating convincing but fraudulent communications that trick administrators into approving unauthorized machine identity access. Strengthening identity verification processes, implementing phishing-resistant authentication methods, and enforcing strict access controls can help mitigate these AI-powered threats.

Adversarial AI is another significant risk to machine identity security, where cybercriminals use AI models to manipulate machine learning-driven security systems. Attackers train adversarial AI models to deceive anomaly detection systems, allowing them to bypass authentication and authorization mechanisms without triggering alerts. For example, AI can generate synthetic API requests that mimic normal behavior, allowing malicious traffic to blend in with legitimate service-to-service communications. This enables attackers to exfiltrate sensitive data, execute privilege escalation attacks, and exploit machine identities undetected. Organizations must enhance their security monitoring capabilities by integrating adaptive AI-driven defense mechanisms that can identify and counter adversarial AI techniques.

Machine learning-powered malware is another emerging threat that targets machine identities. Unlike traditional malware, AI-driven malware continuously learns and adapts to evade detection. These malicious programs can analyze security policies, identify weak authentication mechanisms, and exploit misconfigurations in identity management frameworks. AI-powered malware can also perform automated reconnaissance on machine identities, detecting the best targets for identity spoofing and credential hijacking. To defend against AI-driven malware, organizations must deploy behavioral analytics, endpoint detection and response (EDR) solutions, and AI-powered threat intelligence systems capable of predicting and mitigating evolving attack patterns.

The use of AI in identity spoofing has become increasingly sophisticated, enabling attackers to forge digital certificates, API tokens, and service account credentials. AI-powered tools can generate synthetic identities that closely resemble legitimate machine identities, making it difficult for traditional security systems to distinguish between trusted and malicious entities. Attackers exploit this capability to create rogue microservices, manipulate DevOps pipelines, and infiltrate enterprise environments. Implementing cryptographic verification, certificate pinning, and multi-factor authentication for machine identities can help organizations defend against AI-driven identity forgery.

Another concerning aspect of AI-enabled attacks on machine identities is the automation of lateral movement within networks. Once attackers gain access to a machine identity, AI-driven attack frameworks can autonomously scan internal environments, identify additional vulnerabilities, and exploit interconnected systems without human intervention. AI-powered lateral movement techniques allow cybercriminals to escalate privileges, access sensitive infrastructure, and establish persistent footholds in enterprise environments. Organizations must implement zero trust security models, enforce strict least privilege access policies, and continuously monitor identity activity to detect and block AI-assisted lateral movement.

The increasing reliance on AI in cybersecurity also presents risks related to AI model poisoning and data manipulation. Attackers target machine learning algorithms used for identity verification, modifying training data to introduce security weaknesses. AI model poisoning enables attackers to influence authentication decisions, allowing unauthorized machines to gain access to protected resources. Data integrity attacks can also manipulate identity logs, altering evidence of malicious activity and evading forensic investigations. Organizations must secure AI training datasets, implement model validation techniques, and use cryptographic integrity checks to prevent AI model tampering.

Cloud-based AI systems introduce additional challenges in securing machine identities. Many enterprises use AI-driven cloud services for automation, analytics, and decision-making, but these services require API keys, authentication tokens, and cloud service accounts to function. AI-driven cyberattacks target misconfigured cloud identities, leveraging exposed credentials to gain unauthorized access to AI processing resources. Attackers also exploit AI-driven auto-scaling mechanisms to launch resource exhaustion attacks, forcing cloud services to over-provision resources and incur significant financial costs. Strengthening API security, enforcing identity governance, and implementing cloud-native security controls can help mitigate AI-related threats in cloud environments.

AI also plays a role in automating supply chain attacks, where attackers infiltrate software dependencies, open-source libraries, and CI/CD pipelines to compromise machine identities. AI-powered attack frameworks analyze software repositories for unpatched vulnerabilities, inject malicious code into trusted dependencies, and distribute trojanized machine identities throughout enterprise ecosystems. These attacks are particularly dangerous in DevOps environments, where automated build and deployment processes rely on machine identities to execute tasks. Organizations must secure their software supply chains by implementing code integrity verification, dependency monitoring, and AI-driven anomaly detection systems.

Defensive AI solutions provide organizations with new capabilities to counter AI-driven threats to machine identities. AI-powered security tools analyze vast amounts of identity-related telemetry data, identifying suspicious behavior, unauthorized credential use, and machine identity anomalies in real time. Adaptive AI models continuously learn from new attack techniques, improving their ability to detect previously unknown threats. AI-driven automation enhances incident response by autonomously revoking compromised credentials, blocking malicious API requests, and enforcing identity governance policies. Organizations that leverage AI-driven security solutions can stay ahead of adversaries who use AI to exploit machine identities.

The convergence of artificial intelligence and machine identity security presents both opportunities and challenges for enterprises. While AI-driven cyber threats continue to evolve, AI-powered security measures offer advanced detection, response, and prevention capabilities. Organizations must adopt a proactive approach to securing machine identities by integrating AI-driven defenses, enforcing zero trust principles, and continuously adapting to emerging AI-enabled attack techniques. Strengthening authentication, authorization, and cryptographic verification mechanisms ensures that machine identities remain protected against the sophisticated threats posed by artificial intelligence in the evolving cybersecurity landscape.

Role-Based Access Control (RBAC) for Machine Identities

Role-Based Access Control (RBAC) is a fundamental security mechanism that helps organizations manage permissions efficiently by assigning roles to identities instead of granting direct access to resources. While RBAC has traditionally been used to control human access to IT systems, it has become increasingly critical in managing machine identities. As enterprises adopt cloud computing, DevOps workflows, containerized environments, and microservices architectures, machine identities—including applications, services, APIs, and workloads—require well-defined access controls to prevent unauthorized access and privilege escalation. Without RBAC, machine identities could be overprivileged, leading to security vulnerabilities that attackers can exploit to gain control over sensitive systems.

In an RBAC framework, machine identities are assigned roles that define what actions they can perform and which resources they can access. These roles are mapped to specific permissions that enforce security policies based on predefined access levels. Instead of granting unrestricted access to every machine identity, RBAC ensures that each entity operates within the principle of least privilege, minimizing the risk of security breaches caused by excessive permissions. A machine identity assigned a specific role can only interact with approved resources and execute authorized operations, preventing unauthorized access to critical systems.

RBAC helps mitigate security risks associated with identity sprawl, a common issue in cloud and DevOps environments where thousands of machine identities are created dynamically. When organizations fail to track or restrict machine identities, misconfigured or orphaned credentials can accumulate, providing attackers with unmonitored entry points. By enforcing RBAC policies, enterprises can ensure that every machine identity has a clearly defined role, reducing the likelihood of unauthorized privilege escalation and preventing excessive access to sensitive infrastructure.

In Kubernetes environments, RBAC plays a crucial role in securing machine identities such as pods, controllers, and service accounts. Kubernetes RBAC enables administrators to define roles and bind them to machine identities using role bindings or cluster role bindings. A Kubernetes role defines permissions at the namespace level, while a cluster role applies to the entire cluster. Service accounts assigned to pods inherit RBAC-defined permissions, ensuring that workloads only interact with resources they are authorized to access. By implementing Kubernetes RBAC, organizations can prevent unauthorized service-to-service communication and reduce the attack surface of their containerized workloads.

Cloud platforms also leverage RBAC to manage machine identity permissions effectively. Cloud providers such as AWS, Microsoft Azure, and Google Cloud Platform (GCP) offer built-in IAM roles that allow administrators to define and enforce access controls for machine identities. AWS IAM roles, for example, enable cloud workloads, Lambda functions, and containerized applications to access other AWS services securely. Azure Role-Based Access Control (Azure RBAC) allows administrators to assign roles to service principals, managing machine identity permissions with fine-grained access policies. GCP IAM roles follow a similar approach, ensuring that machine identities within cloud environments operate with the least privilege necessary.

RBAC enhances security by providing centralized policy enforcement and visibility into machine identity activities. Organizations can audit machine identity permissions, track access requests, and detect potential security violations in real time. Security teams can generate reports that highlight overprivileged machine identities, identify unused roles, and ensure that all access policies align with compliance requirements. Implementing continuous monitoring and audit logging enables organizations to detect anomalies, unauthorized role modifications, and potential insider threats before they escalate into security incidents.

The implementation of RBAC for machine identities requires careful role definition and assignment to prevent privilege creep. Organizations should follow a structured approach by categorizing machine identities based on their function and assigning roles that grant only the necessary permissions. For example, an API gateway service should have an API consumer role that allows it to interact with backend services but restricts administrative operations. Similarly, a database workload should have a read-only role if it does not need write permissions, ensuring that unauthorized modifications cannot occur. Regularly reviewing and updating role assignments prevents privilege escalation and enforces least privilege access.

RBAC also helps organizations enforce segregation of duties (SoD), a critical security principle that ensures that no single machine identity has excessive control over multiple sensitive operations. In DevOps pipelines, for instance, separate roles should be assigned for building, testing, and deploying applications. This prevents a single compromised machine identity from executing code changes, approving deployments, and modifying infrastructure configurations simultaneously. By enforcing SoD through RBAC, organizations reduce the risk of insider threats and minimize the impact of security breaches.

Automating RBAC policy enforcement ensures that machine identity permissions remain consistent and secure across dynamic environments. Security teams can integrate RBAC with identity orchestration platforms that automatically assign roles based on predefined templates. These platforms help organizations standardize access controls across cloud services, CI/CD pipelines, Kubernetes clusters, and on-premises infrastructure. Automated role assignment reduces human errors, eliminates manual configuration inconsistencies, and accelerates security policy enforcement in large-scale enterprise environments.

RBAC can also be combined with Attribute-Based Access Control (ABAC) to enhance machine identity security. While RBAC assigns roles based on predefined categories, ABAC evaluates additional attributes such as device type, geolocation, request context, and security posture before granting access. For example, an IoT device may require an identity with a predefined role, but ABAC can restrict its access further based on environmental conditions, such as network location or operational state. By integrating RBAC with ABAC, organizations can create more adaptive security policies that dynamically adjust to evolving threats and business requirements.

Compliance with regulatory frameworks further emphasizes the importance of RBAC for machine identities. Regulations such as GDPR, HIPAA, PCI-DSS, and NIST require organizations to implement strict access controls, enforce least privilege policies, and maintain audit logs of identity-related activities. RBAC provides a structured approach to meeting these compliance requirements by ensuring that machine identities are properly managed and monitored. By enforcing RBAC policies, organizations can demonstrate compliance with industry standards, reduce the risk of regulatory penalties, and improve their overall security posture.

RBAC is a foundational component of machine identity security, ensuring that automated systems, applications, and cloud workloads operate within controlled access boundaries. By enforcing role-based permissions, preventing privilege escalation, integrating with cloud IAM solutions, and automating policy enforcement, organizations can effectively manage machine identity security in complex IT environments. As enterprises continue to scale their digital operations, RBAC remains a critical security mechanism that enables controlled access, mitigates security risks, and maintains compliance with evolving cybersecurity regulations.

Policy-Driven Machine Identity Management

As organizations scale their digital operations, the number of machine identities—such as APIs, cloud workloads, IoT devices, containers, and microservices—continues to grow exponentially. Managing these identities manually is neither efficient nor secure, as it increases the risk of misconfigurations, unauthorized access, and identity sprawl. Policy-driven machine identity management provides a structured approach to automating and enforcing security best practices across distributed environments. By defining policies that govern the issuance, usage, rotation, and revocation of machine identities, organizations can ensure that all machine-to-machine interactions remain secure, compliant, and resilient against emerging cyber threats.

A policy-driven approach establishes clear rules for managing machine identities, ensuring that security teams do not have to manually assign credentials, configure access permissions, or enforce expiration policies. Instead, predefined policies dictate how machine identities should be provisioned and maintained, reducing human error and inconsistencies. These policies define the security requirements for authentication, encryption, and key management, ensuring that machine identities adhere to strict access control mechanisms. By integrating policy-based automation, enterprises can eliminate the risks associated with improperly managed credentials and enforce consistent security standards across their IT infrastructure.

Identity issuance policies govern how machine identities are created and distributed. A well-defined issuance policy ensures that only authorized systems and applications can request new machine identities and that each identity follows a standardized provisioning process. For example, an organization may require all machine identities to be issued through a trusted certificate authority (CA) with predefined validity periods and cryptographic standards. Policies can specify whether an API key, OAuth token, or digital certificate is required based on the security sensitivity of the service requesting authentication. Enforcing strict issuance policies prevents unauthorized machine identities from being created and mitigates the risk of rogue identities infiltrating enterprise environments.

Access control policies define the permissions and privileges granted to each machine identity. These policies ensure that machine identities operate under the principle of least privilege, granting only the minimum necessary access to perform their intended function. Role-based access control (RBAC) and attribute-based access control (ABAC) frameworks help enforce these policies by dynamically assigning permissions based on identity attributes, usage context, and security posture. For example, a machine identity assigned to a cloud database should only have read or write access based on its operational requirements, while an API identity should be restricted to authorized endpoints. Centralizing access control policies allows security teams to enforce consistency and prevent privilege escalation attacks.

Machine identity rotation policies play a critical role in reducing the risk of credential compromise. Static credentials, such as long-lived API keys or SSH keys, pose a significant security risk if they are leaked or stolen. Rotation policies enforce automated key and certificate renewal at predefined intervals, ensuring that even if an identity credential is compromised, its validity is limited. Short-lived credentials, such as just-in-time (JIT) identities, further enhance security by generating temporary authentication tokens that expire after a set duration. Automating credential rotation through policy-driven workflows minimizes the risk of credential theft and ensures that machine identities are continuously updated.

Revocation policies define how and when machine identities should be deactivated. If a machine identity is compromised, orphaned, or no longer required, revocation policies ensure that it is removed from authentication and access control systems. Certificate revocation lists (CRLs) and Online Certificate Status Protocol (OCSP) services enable real-time verification of certificate validity, preventing revoked identities from being used in authentication processes. Automated revocation mechanisms help organizations respond quickly to security incidents by instantly disabling compromised credentials, reducing the risk of unauthorized access and lateral movement within the network.

Policy-driven compliance management helps organizations adhere to regulatory frameworks that require strict identity governance. Regulations such as GDPR, HIPAA, PCI-DSS, and NIST mandate that machine identities follow specific security controls, including encryption, authentication, and logging requirements. Policies can be designed to enforce compliance by ensuring that all machine identities meet regulatory standards before being issued or renewed. Automated policy enforcement tools can generate compliance reports, track identity activity, and provide audit trails that demonstrate adherence to industry regulations. By embedding compliance into machine identity policies, organizations can reduce regulatory risks and avoid penalties for non-compliance.

Monitoring and enforcement of machine identity policies require continuous security visibility. Organizations must implement security information and event management (SIEM) systems to log and analyze machine identity activity in real time. Identity usage analytics help detect anomalies, such as unauthorized access attempts, excessive API calls, or abnormal certificate renewals. Security teams can use policy-driven threat intelligence to identify potential breaches and enforce automated responses, such as revoking suspicious identities or blocking access requests. Proactive monitoring ensures that machine identities remain compliant with security policies and are not exploited by malicious actors.

Policy automation tools integrate with identity and access management (IAM) platforms, certificate authorities, and secrets management solutions to enforce machine identity policies at scale. These tools enable centralized policy orchestration, allowing security teams to define and apply identity governance rules across cloud, on-premises, and hybrid environments. Organizations can integrate policy-driven identity management with cloud-native services such as AWS IAM, Azure Active Directory, and Google Cloud IAM to enforce consistent access control policies across distributed systems. Automating policy enforcement reduces administrative overhead while strengthening the security posture of enterprise infrastructure.

Applying Zero Trust principles to policy-driven machine identity management ensures that no machine identity is implicitly trusted. Instead, continuous authentication and authorization checks are enforced through policy-driven frameworks that validate machine identities in real time. Conditional access policies can be used to grant or deny access based on contextual factors such as network location, device security posture, or behavioral analytics. By combining Zero Trust with policy automation, organizations can dynamically adjust machine identity access privileges based on evolving security conditions, minimizing the risk of unauthorized access and privilege escalation.

Scalability is a key advantage of policy-driven machine identity management, allowing enterprises to manage millions of machine identities across complex IT environments. Manual identity management processes become increasingly unmanageable as organizations scale their cloud workloads, IoT devices, and microservices. Policy-driven frameworks enable organizations to automate the lifecycle management of machine identities, ensuring that issuance, rotation, and revocation processes remain consistent regardless of the scale of operations. By integrating identity management policies with DevOps and CI/CD pipelines, organizations can ensure that machine identities are provisioned securely without disrupting development and deployment workflows.

Organizations must continuously refine and update machine identity policies to address evolving cybersecurity threats. Threat actors constantly develop new techniques to exploit identity weaknesses, requiring enterprises to adopt adaptive security policies that evolve alongside emerging risks. Machine learning-driven analytics can enhance policy enforcement by identifying patterns of suspicious behavior and automatically adjusting identity privileges based on real-time risk assessments. By adopting an adaptive policy-driven approach, organizations can proactively defend against machine identity threats while maintaining operational agility.

Policy-driven machine identity management is essential for securing modern IT environments, ensuring compliance, and mitigating identity-related threats. By automating identity issuance, enforcing strict access controls, rotating credentials, revoking unused identities, and integrating continuous monitoring, organizations can protect machine identities from exploitation. Implementing a robust policy framework enables enterprises to manage machine identities efficiently, scale security operations, and maintain trust in their digital infrastructure.

Secrets Management and Secure Storage Solutions

Secrets management has become a critical component of modern security frameworks as organizations increasingly rely on machine identities, automation, and cloud-based applications. Secrets such as API keys, authentication tokens, encryption keys, digital certificates, and database credentials are essential for enabling secure machine-to-machine communication. However, improper management of these secrets can lead to unauthorized access, credential leaks, and system compromise. As organizations scale their IT infrastructure, they must implement secure storage solutions and best practices to protect sensitive credentials from being exposed, stolen, or misused.

One of the primary challenges in secrets management is preventing secrets from being hardcoded into source code, configuration files, or log files. Developers often embed credentials directly within application code for convenience, but this practice significantly increases security risks. If a repository containing hardcoded secrets is accidentally made public or accessed by an unauthorized party, attackers can exploit these credentials to gain access to critical systems. Organizations must enforce strict policies that prohibit hardcoded secrets and integrate automated scanning tools to detect and remove exposed credentials before they are committed to version control systems.

Secure storage solutions provide a centralized approach to managing and protecting secrets. Secrets management platforms such as HashiCorp Vault, AWS Secrets Manager, Azure Key Vault, and Google Secret Manager offer dedicated infrastructure for storing, retrieving, and rotating secrets. These solutions provide encryption at rest and in transit, ensuring that secrets remain protected from unauthorized access. By integrating secure storage solutions with identity and access management (IAM) frameworks, organizations can enforce granular access controls that restrict which applications, services, and users can retrieve specific secrets.

Automated secret rotation is a crucial practice for minimizing the risk of credential compromise. Long-lived secrets increase the likelihood of unauthorized use, as attackers who obtain static credentials can use them indefinitely. Automated rotation policies enforce periodic updates to API keys, database passwords, and authentication tokens, ensuring that secrets remain valid only for a limited duration. Short-lived credentials, such as temporary security tokens generated by cloud IAM services, further reduce the risk of credential exposure. Implementing just-in-time (JIT) access mechanisms ensures that secrets are only issued when needed and revoked immediately after use, reducing the attack surface.

Access control policies play a fundamental role in protecting secrets. Least privilege access ensures that only authorized identities, applications, and services can retrieve specific secrets. Role-based access control (RBAC) and attribute-based access control (ABAC) frameworks enforce fine-grained permissions, preventing overprivileged access to sensitive credentials. By defining access policies based on contextual factors such as workload identity, device security posture, and geographic location, organizations can restrict access to secrets dynamically. Integrating multi-factor authentication (MFA) and conditional access policies further strengthens security by requiring additional verification before secrets can be retrieved.

Encryption is essential for securing secrets at rest and in transit. Secrets stored in plaintext are vulnerable to data breaches, insider threats, and unauthorized access. Secure storage solutions use strong encryption algorithms such as AES-256 to protect stored secrets, ensuring that even if an attacker gains access to the storage system, they cannot decrypt the credentials without the proper encryption keys. Transport Layer Security (TLS) encrypts secrets in transit, preventing interception during retrieval. Organizations must also implement hardware security modules (HSMs) for managing encryption keys securely, ensuring that cryptographic operations are isolated from unauthorized access.

Audit logging and monitoring provide visibility into secret usage and access attempts. Security teams must track which identities access specific secrets, when access occurs, and whether any unauthorized attempts are detected. Logging solutions integrate with security information and event management (SIEM) systems to aggregate and analyze secret-related events in real time. Anomalous access patterns, such as unexpected access attempts from unknown locations or excessive secret retrievals, can indicate a security breach. Implementing anomaly detection and automated response mechanisms ensures that compromised secrets are revoked immediately, reducing potential damage.

Secrets management in containerized environments presents unique challenges, as containers frequently start, stop, and scale dynamically. Kubernetes provides native secret management capabilities, but by default, Kubernetes secrets are stored in etcd without encryption. Organizations must enforce encryption for Kubernetes secrets at rest and integrate external secret management solutions to enhance security. Service meshes such as Istio provide additional security layers by enabling mutual TLS (mTLS) for encrypted service-to-service communication, ensuring that secrets remain protected in distributed microservices architectures.

Cloud-native applications require secrets management solutions that integrate seamlessly with cloud platforms. Cloud providers offer built-in secret storage services that allow applications to retrieve secrets securely without exposing them in configuration files or environment variables. AWS Secrets Manager and Azure Key Vault provide policy-driven access control, automatic secret rotation, and audit logging capabilities that enhance security in cloud deployments. By leveraging cloud-native secrets management, organizations can ensure that machine identities and workloads access credentials securely without increasing administrative overhead.

The adoption of Infrastructure as Code (IaC) introduces additional considerations for secrets management. IaC tools such as Terraform, Ansible, and CloudFormation enable automated provisioning of infrastructure resources, but improperly managing secrets in IaC templates can lead to credential leaks. Organizations must avoid storing secrets in plaintext within configuration files and instead use secure reference mechanisms that retrieve secrets dynamically from vaults. Implementing automated security scans for IaC templates helps detect exposed credentials before they are deployed, reducing the risk of misconfiguration.

Zero trust security models reinforce the importance of strict secrets management policies. In a zero trust architecture, no machine identity or application is inherently trusted, and access to secrets must be continuously verified based on policy enforcement. Conditional access policies evaluate contextual factors such as workload behavior, threat intelligence, and real-time risk assessments before granting access to secrets. By enforcing zero trust principles, organizations can minimize the impact of credential leaks and prevent unauthorized machine identities from misusing secrets.

Compliance and regulatory frameworks mandate strong secrets management practices to protect sensitive data and ensure compliance with security standards. Regulations such as GDPR, HIPAA, PCI-DSS, and NIST require organizations to enforce encryption, access controls, and audit logging for credential storage. Policy-driven secrets management ensures that organizations maintain compliance by enforcing standardized security measures across all environments. Automated compliance reporting and audit trails help organizations demonstrate adherence to security requirements while reducing the risk of regulatory penalties.

Threat actors actively target secrets as a means of gaining unauthorized access to enterprise systems. Credential stuffing attacks, API key theft, and secret leakage in public repositories are common attack vectors that can lead to severe security breaches. Implementing a comprehensive secrets management strategy that includes automated secret rotation, encryption, access control enforcement, monitoring, and compliance integration is essential for mitigating these risks. Organizations must continuously evaluate and improve their secrets management practices to keep pace with evolving cyber threats.

Secrets management and secure storage solutions are fundamental to protecting machine identities, preventing unauthorized access, and ensuring the integrity of digital operations. By leveraging automated secret storage, enforcing strict access controls, integrating encryption, monitoring secret access, and aligning with compliance requirements, organizations can build a resilient security framework that safeguards their machine identities and critical systems from credential-based attacks.

Identifying and Mitigating Machine Identity Sprawl

Machine identity sprawl has become a significant security concern as organizations increasingly rely on cloud environments, DevOps automation, IoT devices, and microservices architectures. Unlike human identities, which are managed through user authentication and access control, machine identities are often created, used, and forgotten without a structured management process. This uncontrolled proliferation of machine identities—such as API keys, digital certificates, service accounts, and cryptographic credentials—leads to identity sprawl, where organizations lose visibility over which systems are using which credentials. The risk associated with machine identity sprawl is substantial, as untracked, misconfigured, or orphaned identities can be exploited by attackers to gain unauthorized access, move laterally within networks, and escalate privileges. Organizations must implement proactive strategies to identify, control, and mitigate machine identity sprawl to maintain a strong security posture.

One of the primary causes of machine identity sprawl is the rapid adoption of cloud computing and DevOps workflows, where automated systems generate new identities at an unprecedented scale. In cloud-native environments, virtual machines, containers, and serverless functions frequently create temporary machine identities for authentication and authorization purposes. Without a centralized management framework, these identities accumulate over time, leading to security blind spots. Developers and DevOps teams often generate API keys, OAuth tokens, and SSH credentials for automation tasks but fail to track their usage or enforce expiration policies. This results in abandoned or stale credentials that remain valid, increasing the attack surface for potential breaches.

Organizations must first gain visibility into their existing machine identities to identify sprawl effectively. A comprehensive inventory of all machine identities, their associated credentials, and their usage patterns is essential for understanding the scope of the problem. Security teams should conduct audits to locate digital certificates, API keys, secrets, and service accounts across cloud environments, on-premises infrastructure, and DevOps pipelines. Automated discovery tools help scan repositories, logs, and configuration files to detect hardcoded or orphaned credentials that may have been forgotten. By creating a real-time inventory, organizations can assess how many machine identities exist, where they are being used, and whether they comply with security policies.

Once machine identities have been identified, organizations must categorize them based on their risk level and criticality. High-risk machine identities—such as those with administrative privileges, access to sensitive data, or elevated permissions—must be prioritized for remediation. Identities that have not been used in an extended period should be flagged for review, while those that are no longer associated with an active workload must be revoked. Security teams should define retention policies that determine the lifespan of machine identities based on their purpose, ensuring that unnecessary credentials are decommissioned automatically to prevent identity accumulation.

Mitigating machine identity sprawl requires enforcing strict governance policies that regulate identity issuance, rotation, and expiration. Role-based access control (RBAC) and attribute-based access control (ABAC) frameworks should be implemented to restrict which users, applications, and systems can create and manage machine identities. Machine identity creation should follow a policy-driven approach where security teams define approval workflows, ensuring that new credentials are generated only when necessary and assigned appropriate permissions. Enforcing least privilege access prevents overprivileged identities from being misused, reducing the risk of identity compromise.

Automated lifecycle management is crucial in mitigating machine identity sprawl. Identity lifecycle automation solutions integrate with cloud IAM platforms, certificate authorities, and secrets management tools to ensure that machine identities follow standardized security best practices. Organizations should implement automated workflows for credential rotation, certificate renewal, and key expiration to prevent the accumulation of stale identities. Just-in-time (JIT) access provisioning further reduces identity sprawl by granting machine identities temporary credentials that expire after a defined period, ensuring that long-lived credentials do not persist unnecessarily.

Continuous monitoring and anomaly detection play a vital role in identifying machine identity misuse and security gaps. Security information and event management (SIEM) systems aggregate identity-related logs, allowing organizations to detect suspicious activity, such as unexpected API key usage, excessive service account access, or abnormal authentication patterns. Machine learning-driven behavioral analytics can help identify anomalies in machine identity usage, flagging credentials that may have been compromised or used outside of their intended scope. Real-time alerting enables security teams to respond proactively by revoking misused credentials and preventing unauthorized access.

Implementing a centralized machine identity management platform provides organizations with visibility, control, and enforcement capabilities to prevent sprawl. A dedicated identity orchestration system consolidates machine identity governance across multi-cloud, hybrid, and on-premises environments, ensuring that security policies remain consistent. Organizations should integrate identity management solutions with existing security frameworks, including IAM platforms, API gateways, and certificate management tools, to streamline identity tracking and policy enforcement. Standardizing identity management practices reduces complexity and minimizes the risk of security misconfigurations.

Zero trust security models further enhance machine identity sprawl mitigation by enforcing continuous authentication and authorization for all machine-to-machine interactions. Under zero trust principles, machine identities are not inherently trusted, and access requests are validated dynamically based on contextual risk assessments. Conditional access policies evaluate real-time factors, such as workload behavior, location, and access frequency, before granting machine identities permission to interact with enterprise systems. Enforcing zero trust policies ensures that machine identities remain under strict security controls, reducing the risk of abandoned or misused credentials.

Compliance and regulatory frameworks emphasize the importance of machine identity governance to maintain data protection and security standards. Regulations such as GDPR, HIPAA, PCI-DSS, and NIST require organizations to enforce strong identity authentication, access controls, and audit logging for all digital interactions. Machine identity sprawl poses a compliance risk, as untracked identities may fail to meet regulatory requirements. By maintaining a structured machine identity governance model, organizations can demonstrate compliance through automated reporting, audit trails, and real-time monitoring of identity usage.

Reducing machine identity sprawl also involves educating developers, DevOps teams, and security personnel on best practices for identity management. Awareness training programs should emphasize the risks of credential overuse, hardcoded secrets, and excessive identity privileges. Developers should be encouraged to use secrets management tools rather than embedding credentials in code repositories, and security teams should conduct periodic reviews of machine identity policies to identify areas for improvement. Fostering a security-conscious culture helps organizations prevent identity mismanagement and reduce the likelihood of identity-related security incidents.

Machine identity sprawl is a growing security challenge that requires proactive identification, governance, and mitigation strategies. By gaining visibility into machine identities, enforcing automated lifecycle management, implementing least privilege access controls, and leveraging centralized identity management solutions, organizations can prevent unauthorized identity accumulation and strengthen their security posture. Integrating zero trust principles, continuous monitoring, and compliance frameworks further ensures that machine identities remain secure, traceable, and compliant in an increasingly complex digital landscape.

Auditing and Monitoring Machine Identities

The growing reliance on machine identities to facilitate authentication, encryption, and access control across enterprise environments has made auditing and monitoring these identities a critical aspect of cybersecurity. Machine identities, including digital certificates, API keys, SSH keys, and cloud service accounts, are essential for securing machine-to-machine interactions. However, without continuous auditing and monitoring, organizations risk identity misuse, unauthorized access, and credential compromise. Attackers actively target mismanaged machine identities to gain unauthorized control over critical infrastructure, making it imperative for organizations to implement a robust auditing and monitoring framework that provides visibility, control, and real-time threat detection.

Auditing machine identities involves systematically reviewing identity usage, permissions, and security policies to ensure compliance with best practices and regulatory requirements. A comprehensive audit helps organizations understand how machine identities are issued, where they are used, and whether they adhere to security policies. Regular audits prevent identity sprawl by identifying and decommissioning stale, orphaned, or misconfigured credentials that could be exploited by attackers. By maintaining an up-to-date inventory of machine identities, security teams can enforce governance policies and mitigate risks associated with unauthorized credential access.

A key aspect of auditing machine identities is analyzing access logs to track authentication attempts and privilege escalations. Every interaction involving a machine identity should be logged, allowing security teams to investigate potential anomalies, such as unauthorized access requests, excessive API calls, or unexpected certificate usage. Security information and event management (SIEM) solutions aggregate identity-related logs from across the enterprise, providing real-time visibility into machine identity activity. Advanced logging mechanisms capture authentication events, credential usage patterns, and failed access attempts, enabling security teams to detect suspicious behavior before it escalates into a security breach.

Monitoring machine identities requires continuous observation of identity behavior to detect potential security threats. Machine identities should be monitored for deviations from normal activity, such as identities accessing resources they do not typically interact with or credentials being used from unexpected geographic locations. Behavioral analytics and artificial intelligence (AI)-driven anomaly detection systems analyze historical identity usage patterns to establish baselines, flagging deviations that indicate potential compromise. By leveraging machine learning models, security teams can identify identity misuse that would otherwise go undetected by traditional rule-based monitoring approaches.

Certificate monitoring is an essential component of machine identity management, as expired or misconfigured certificates can lead to service outages and authentication failures. Digital certificates enable encrypted communication between machines, but if they are not properly monitored, they can introduce security vulnerabilities. Automated certificate monitoring solutions track certificate expiration dates, renewal processes, and revocation statuses, ensuring that expired certificates are replaced before they cause disruptions. Monitoring certificate authorities (CAs) for unauthorized certificate issuance helps prevent certificate-based attacks, such as man-in-the-middle (MITM) attacks and domain impersonation attempts.

Machine identity monitoring extends beyond individual credentials to include monitoring service-to-service communication patterns. Modern enterprise environments rely on APIs, microservices, and cloud workloads that authenticate using machine identities.

Monitoring API traffic helps detect unauthorized service requests, excessive credential usage, and potential API abuse. API gateways and service meshes provide visibility into service-to-service authentication, enforcing identity-based access policies to prevent malicious interactions. By continuously monitoring API interactions, organizations can prevent unauthorized data access, detect anomalous API usage, and enforce machine identity governance policies.

Cloud-based machine identity monitoring presents unique challenges due to the dynamic nature of cloud workloads. Cloud instances, serverless functions, and containers generate temporary machine identities that require continuous monitoring to ensure they are not misused. Cloud-native security tools such as AWS CloudTrail, Azure Monitor, and Google Cloud Logging provide event-driven monitoring capabilities that track identity authentication, privilege changes, and API interactions across cloud environments. Integrating cloud identity monitoring with centralized security analytics platforms ensures that organizations maintain visibility into identity usage across multi-cloud and hybrid infrastructures.

Auditing machine identity permissions is essential for enforcing the principle of least privilege. Overprivileged machine identities pose a significant security risk, as they can be exploited by attackers to gain unauthorized control over sensitive resources. Security teams must regularly review access control lists (ACLs), IAM role assignments, and service account permissions to identify excessive privileges. Automated identity access reviews help enforce policy-based restrictions, revoking unnecessary permissions and ensuring that machine identities are granted only the access necessary for their intended functions.

Threat intelligence integration enhances machine identity monitoring by correlating identity-related activity with known attack indicators. Cyber threat intelligence feeds provide real-time updates on credential theft campaigns, compromised identity repositories, and machine identity abuse tactics used by threat actors. Security teams can use these insights to proactively identify suspicious identity activity, block unauthorized authentication attempts, and respond to emerging threats before they impact enterprise systems. By integrating threat intelligence with identity monitoring platforms, organizations strengthen their ability to detect and mitigate identity-based attacks.

Incident response automation plays a critical role in mitigating machine identity threats detected through auditing and monitoring. When an identity-related security event is detected, automated response mechanisms can revoke compromised credentials, block unauthorized access requests, and trigger forensic investigations. Security orchestration, automation, and response (SOAR) platforms integrate with identity monitoring tools to enforce real-time security policies, reducing the time it takes to respond to machine identity breaches. By automating incident response workflows, organizations can minimize the impact of identity-related attacks while ensuring rapid remediation of security incidents.

Regulatory compliance mandates strict auditing and monitoring of machine identities to protect sensitive data and prevent unauthorized access. Regulations such as GDPR, HIPAA, PCI-DSS, and NIST require organizations to implement logging, access reviews, and real-time monitoring of identity usage. Compliance audits verify that machine identity management practices align with industry standards, ensuring that credentials are properly secured and that unauthorized access attempts are logged and investigated. Automated compliance reporting tools generate audit logs that provide evidence of identity governance, helping organizations demonstrate regulatory adherence while improving overall security posture.

Continuous improvement is necessary to maintain effective auditing and monitoring of machine identities. Organizations must refine their identity monitoring strategies based on evolving security threats, emerging technologies, and lessons learned from past incidents. Regular security assessments, penetration testing, and red teaming exercises help identify weaknesses in machine identity controls, enabling security teams to implement proactive measures. By continuously enhancing identity monitoring capabilities, organizations can stay ahead of attackers and maintain robust security defenses in an increasingly complex digital landscape.

A strong auditing and monitoring framework for machine identities provides organizations with the visibility and control needed to prevent unauthorized access, detect suspicious activity, and enforce compliance. By implementing continuous identity monitoring, leveraging behavioral analytics, integrating threat intelligence, automating incident response, and conducting regular access audits, enterprises can strengthen their security posture and reduce the risk of machine identity-related breaches. Organizations that prioritize proactive auditing and real-time monitoring of machine identities gain a significant advantage in securing their digital ecosystems against emerging cyber threats.

Threat Detection for Compromised Machine Identities

Machine identities play a crucial role in securing enterprise environments by enabling authentication, encryption, and access control for automated systems, cloud workloads, APIs, and microservices. However, as organizations increasingly rely on machine identities to facilitate digital operations, attackers have adapted their tactics to exploit vulnerabilities in identity management. Compromised machine identities present a significant security risk, as attackers can use stolen credentials, digital certificates, API keys, or service accounts to gain unauthorized access, escalate privileges, and move laterally within networks undetected. Effective threat detection mechanisms are essential to identifying and mitigating the risks associated with compromised machine identities before they result in major security breaches.

One of the primary indicators of a compromised machine identity is anomalous authentication behavior. Machine identities typically follow predictable authentication patterns, such as accessing the same set of resources at regular intervals or authenticating from known IP addresses. When an identity suddenly exhibits unusual authentication attempts—such as accessing resources outside its normal scope, authenticating from a foreign geographic location, or making an excessive number of login requests—it may indicate that the identity has been compromised. Security teams must implement real-time authentication monitoring to detect deviations from normal identity behavior and take immediate action to investigate and mitigate potential threats.

Lateral movement is a common tactic used by attackers who have gained access to a compromised machine identity. Instead of launching immediate attacks, adversaries often explore the network, searching for higher-value targets and additional credentials that can be exploited. Monitoring machine identity activity for unauthorized privilege escalations, excessive resource access requests, or attempts to communicate with previously uncontacted services can help detect lateral movement. Identity-based anomaly detection systems use machine learning algorithms to establish behavioral baselines and flag suspicious deviations that may indicate identity compromise. By continuously monitoring service-to-service interactions, organizations can detect unauthorized machine identity usage before an attacker fully exploits network access.

Unauthorized API activity is another critical indicator of compromised machine identities. Many modern applications rely on API keys and OAuth tokens for authentication between services, but if these credentials are leaked, attackers can use them to impersonate trusted services. Threat actors often target API endpoints to extract sensitive data, manipulate business logic, or inject malicious payloads. Monitoring API traffic for unexpected requests, abnormal data transfers, or unauthorized attempts to invoke administrative functions can reveal signs of API key compromise. API gateways and web application firewalls (WAFs) provide visibility into API traffic, enabling security teams to detect suspicious behavior and revoke compromised API keys before attackers can exploit them further.

Excessive certificate use or unexpected certificate issuance may also indicate a machine identity compromise. Digital certificates provide authentication for secure communications, but if an attacker gains access to a valid certificate or forges one through a compromised certificate authority (CA), they can impersonate legitimate services to intercept encrypted data. Monitoring certificate usage across enterprise networks helps identify cases where a certificate is being used on an unexpected system, accessed more frequently than usual, or renewed outside normal scheduling processes. Automated certificate lifecycle management tools help enforce certificate issuance policies, ensuring that only authorized entities can request and renew certificates.

Behavioral analytics enhance threat detection by correlating machine identity activity with known attack patterns. AI-powered security analytics platforms analyze identity usage across multiple dimensions, such as authentication frequency, request patterns, and resource access history, to detect deviations from established baselines. When an identity exhibits behavior that closely matches historical threat intelligence indicators, the system can trigger alerts, allowing security teams to investigate potential compromises. Behavioral-based detection is particularly effective against sophisticated attackers who attempt to disguise their actions within normal network traffic.

Compromised machine identities are often used in credential stuffing attacks, where attackers test large volumes of stolen or guessed credentials across multiple systems to gain unauthorized access. Monitoring failed authentication attempts and identifying patterns of repeated login failures from different locations or IP addresses can indicate an ongoing credential stuffing attack. Rate limiting and automated threat response mechanisms can block excessive login attempts, preventing attackers from exploiting compromised machine identities. Integrating security information and event management (SIEM) systems with identity and access management (IAM) platforms allows security teams to correlate authentication failures with potential brute-force or credential reuse attempts.

Cloud-based machine identities introduce additional security risks, as attackers increasingly target cloud workloads and service accounts to gain access to enterprise infrastructure. Cloud identity monitoring solutions track IAM role usage, privilege escalations, and access patterns to detect potential threats. Unauthorized API calls, unexpected resource provisioning, or deviations in cloud service account behavior may indicate a machine identity compromise. Cloud-native security tools such as AWS GuardDuty, Azure Defender, and Google Cloud Security Command Center provide real-time monitoring and automated alerts for suspicious activity related to machine identities.

Threat intelligence feeds help organizations stay ahead of emerging machine identity attacks by providing real-time data on compromised credentials, malicious IP addresses, and attack techniques. Integrating external threat intelligence with machine identity monitoring systems enhances detection capabilities by identifying known attack indicators before they impact enterprise environments. Threat intelligence platforms aggregate information from global security researchers, government agencies, and industry partners, enabling security teams to proactively block malicious machine identities, revoke compromised credentials, and strengthen identity security policies.

Incident response automation is essential for mitigating the risks associated with compromised machine identities. When a threat is detected, automated response mechanisms can revoke access tokens, disable service accounts, rotate compromised keys, or quarantine affected workloads. Security orchestration, automation, and response (SOAR) platforms streamline incident management by enforcing predefined response workflows, ensuring that compromised machine identities are remediated quickly. Automated containment strategies help prevent attackers from using compromised identities to escalate privileges or move laterally within enterprise networks.

Regulatory compliance frameworks such as GDPR, HIPAA, PCI-DSS, and NIST emphasize the importance of detecting and mitigating identity-related threats to protect sensitive data and prevent unauthorized access. Organizations must implement auditing and monitoring mechanisms that provide real-time visibility into machine identity activity, ensuring compliance with security policies and regulatory requirements. Automated compliance reporting tools generate detailed audit logs that track identity access, authentication attempts, and security incidents, helping organizations maintain transparency and accountability in identity management.

Continuous improvement in machine identity threat detection requires organizations to refine security policies, update behavioral models, and incorporate lessons learned from past incidents. Red teaming exercises, penetration testing, and simulated attack scenarios help evaluate the effectiveness of machine identity monitoring and response capabilities. By continuously testing and evolving threat detection strategies, organizations can stay ahead of attackers and strengthen their defenses against machine identity compromises.

Organizations that prioritize threat detection for compromised machine identities can prevent unauthorized access, minimize security risks, and maintain trust in their digital infrastructure. By leveraging real-time monitoring, behavioral analytics, threat intelligence, and automated incident response, enterprises can detect identity-based threats before they escalate into full-scale security breaches. Implementing a proactive machine identity security strategy ensures that authentication mechanisms remain resilient, access controls are enforced, and attackers are prevented from exploiting machine identities to compromise enterprise systems.

Incident Response and Recovery for Machine Identity Breaches

Machine identity breaches pose a significant risk to enterprise security, as they enable attackers to impersonate trusted services, escalate privileges, and gain unauthorized access to critical systems. Machine identities, including API keys, service accounts, SSH keys, and digital certificates, play a crucial role in securing automated processes and machine-to-machine communication. When these identities are compromised, organizations must act swiftly to contain the threat, revoke affected credentials, and restore trust in their digital infrastructure. A well-defined incident response and recovery strategy is essential to mitigating the impact of machine identity breaches and preventing future attacks.

The first step in responding to a machine identity breach is detection. Security teams must have visibility into all machine identities, authentication events, and access logs to identify signs of compromise. Suspicious activities such as unauthorized access attempts, unexpected certificate usage, excessive API calls, or lateral movement across systems may indicate that a machine identity has been compromised. Security information and event management (SIEM) platforms, cloud-native security tools, and behavioral analytics systems help detect anomalies by correlating identity-related events with known attack patterns. Automated threat intelligence feeds provide additional context by flagging machine identities associated with known malicious activity.

Once a potential breach is detected, security teams must immediately assess the scope of the incident. Identifying which machine identities have been compromised, what resources they accessed, and how the attacker exploited them is critical for containment. Forensic analysis of logs, authentication records, and system activity helps determine the origin of the breach and the extent of the attack. If attackers used stolen API keys or authentication tokens, security teams must trace their activity to identify affected services and data. If a digital certificate was compromised, it is necessary to check whether it was used for unauthorized encryption or impersonation.

Containment is the next critical phase in incident response, aimed at preventing further damage. Revoking compromised credentials, disabling affected service accounts, and enforcing access control restrictions help limit an attacker's ability to continue using machine identities for malicious purposes. Automated identity revocation ensures that compromised credentials are immediately invalidated, reducing the risk of ongoing exploitation. In cloud environments, organizations can use just-in-time (JIT) access controls to temporarily restrict machine identity usage while investigating the breach. Implementing firewall rules, network segmentation, and service isolation prevents attackers from moving laterally across infrastructure and escalating their privileges.

Remediation efforts must focus on identifying and closing security gaps that led to the breach. If an API key was exposed due to hardcoded credentials in source code repositories, security teams should enforce secret scanning tools and implement automated credential rotation policies. If an attacker exploited weak machine identity permissions, organizations should review and tighten access control policies, ensuring that least privilege principles are enforced. In cases where a certificate authority (CA) was compromised, security teams may need to revoke and reissue digital certificates across multiple systems, ensuring that trust chains remain intact.

Recovery involves restoring normal operations while ensuring that machine identities are secured against future threats. Organizations must regenerate and distribute new credentials, reconfigure access permissions, and validate that security policies are correctly enforced. Continuous monitoring of newly issued machine identities helps detect any lingering threats or attempts to reuse revoked credentials. Security teams should conduct post-incident reviews to analyze how the breach occurred, evaluate response effectiveness, and implement long-term security improvements. Strengthening machine identity governance through policy-driven automation ensures that identity-related risks are minimized going forward.

A key aspect of machine identity recovery is certificate lifecycle management. If attackers gained access to private keys, organizations must revoke affected certificates and issue new ones through a trusted CA. Certificate transparency logs help verify whether unauthorized certificates were issued during the breach. Implementing automated certificate renewal ensures that compromised certificates are replaced quickly, minimizing service disruptions. Organizations should also enforce mutual TLS (mTLS) authentication, requiring both client and server verification before establishing encrypted connections.

Cloud-native machine identity recovery requires additional considerations due to the dynamic nature of cloud workloads. If a cloud service account was compromised, organizations must rotate associated IAM credentials, revoke unused permissions, and implement identity federation to reduce reliance on long-lived credentials. Cloud security posture management (CSPM) tools help enforce best practices by identifying misconfigured machine identities and automatically remediating vulnerabilities. Security teams should also review API activity logs to detect unauthorized service-to-service communication and adjust API gateway policies to restrict excessive privilege escalation.

Automating incident response accelerates containment and recovery efforts by reducing the time required to revoke compromised credentials and reestablish security controls. Security orchestration, automation, and response (SOAR) platforms integrate with identity and access management (IAM) systems to enforce predefined remediation workflows. Automated responses can include rotating API keys, disabling affected service accounts, enforcing temporary access restrictions, and triggering forensic analysis reports. By leveraging automation, organizations can minimize manual intervention, improve response time, and reduce the risk of human error during security incidents.

Threat intelligence plays a critical role in machine identity incident response by providing insights into emerging attack techniques and compromised identity trends. Security teams must integrate real-time threat intelligence feeds with identity monitoring tools to detect signs of machine identity abuse early. If an attacker is known to target a specific type of authentication token or exploit a common misconfiguration, proactive security measures can be implemented to prevent similar incidents. Sharing threat intelligence with industry partners and security organizations helps strengthen collective defense strategies against machine identity threats.

Compliance and regulatory requirements mandate organizations to have formal incident response and recovery plans for machine identity breaches. Regulations such as GDPR, HIPAA, PCI-DSS, and NIST require detailed audit logs, incident reporting, and post-breach mitigation measures. Organizations must ensure that they document all actions taken during an incident, including identity revocation, forensic analysis, and remediation efforts. Automated compliance reporting tools streamline regulatory adherence by generating detailed reports on incident response activities, helping organizations demonstrate due diligence and accountability.

Post-incident lessons learned are essential for continuously improving machine identity security. Conducting tabletop exercises, penetration tests, and red teaming assessments helps validate incident response procedures and identify potential weaknesses. Organizations should update machine identity policies based on insights gained from past breaches, ensuring that new threats are addressed before they can be exploited. Training DevOps teams, security engineers, and IT administrators on machine identity best practices fosters a security-first culture that prioritizes proactive threat mitigation.

Organizations that establish a comprehensive incident response and recovery strategy for machine identity breaches can reduce the risk of long-term security compromise, minimize operational disruptions, and strengthen their overall cybersecurity posture. By implementing real-time monitoring, automated identity governance, proactive threat detection, and compliance-driven remediation, enterprises can effectively respond to identity-based attacks and restore trust in their digital ecosystem. Security teams must remain vigilant, continuously refining their incident response playbooks to keep pace with the evolving threat landscape and ensure that machine identities remain protected against unauthorized access and exploitation.

Compliance Requirements and Regulatory Standards

Compliance requirements and regulatory standards play a critical role in defining how organizations must manage machine identities to ensure security, data protection, and adherence to industry regulations. As enterprises increasingly rely on machine identities for authentication, encryption, and access control in cloud environments, DevOps pipelines, and digital transactions, compliance frameworks establish mandatory security controls that must be followed. Failure to comply with these standards can result in regulatory penalties, reputational damage, and increased vulnerability to security breaches. Organizations must align their machine identity management practices with regulatory requirements to maintain trust, mitigate risks, and meet legal obligations.

Regulatory standards vary across industries and geographic regions, but they generally mandate strong authentication mechanisms, identity governance policies, and encryption practices for protecting machine identities. The General Data Protection Regulation (GDPR), for example, requires organizations to implement security measures that protect the integrity and confidentiality of personal data, including enforcing authentication controls for APIs, cloud services, and machine-to-machine communications. GDPR mandates that organizations maintain detailed audit logs of identity-related activity, ensuring that machine identities used for processing personal data are monitored and managed securely. Non-compliance with GDPR can result in significant financial penalties, making it imperative for enterprises to implement strict identity security policies.

The Health Insurance Portability and Accountability Act (HIPAA) establishes compliance requirements for protecting healthcare data and ensuring that only authorized entities can access electronic protected health information (ePHI). Machine identities used in healthcare applications, medical devices, and cloud-based patient record systems must be secured to prevent unauthorized access and data breaches. HIPAA requires encryption for data in transit and at rest, meaning that digital certificates, cryptographic keys, and API credentials must be managed effectively to maintain compliance. Organizations operating in the healthcare sector must enforce strict access control policies, ensuring that machine identities cannot be exploited to gain unauthorized access to sensitive patient information.

The Payment Card Industry Data Security Standard (PCI-DSS) sets forth stringent requirements for securing machine identities involved in payment transactions and financial services. PCI-DSS mandates that all authentication credentials, including API keys and digital certificates, be protected through encryption and access controls. The framework also requires regular security assessments, penetration testing, and audit logging to detect unauthorized identity usage. Machine identities used for processing payment transactions must be rotated periodically, ensuring that compromised credentials cannot be exploited for fraudulent activities. Organizations in the financial sector must implement automated certificate management, secure API authentication, and strict privilege access controls to remain compliant with PCI-DSS.

The National Institute of Standards and Technology (NIST) provides comprehensive security frameworks for managing machine identities, including guidelines on identity and access management (IAM), cryptographic key management, and authentication best practices. NIST Special Publication 800-63 outlines identity verification standards that apply to machine identities in government systems and enterprise IT environments. The NIST Cybersecurity Framework (CSF) recommends continuous monitoring of identity activity, enforcing least privilege access, and implementing automated certificate lifecycle management to mitigate identity-related security risks. Organizations that adopt NIST guidelines benefit from a structured approach to machine identity governance, reducing the likelihood of identity-based attacks and compliance violations.

In cloud computing environments, compliance with identity security standards is essential for protecting workloads, securing service-to-service communications, and preventing unauthorized access. Cloud providers such as Amazon Web Services (AWS), Microsoft Azure, and Google Cloud Platform (GCP) offer identity and access management (IAM) solutions that help organizations enforce compliance with regulatory frameworks. AWS IAM roles, Azure Managed Identities, and GCP Service Accounts allow organizations to manage machine identities securely by defining access policies, enforcing role-based authentication, and implementing key rotation strategies. Compliance certifications such as ISO 27001, SOC 2, and FedRAMP require cloud service providers and enterprises to demonstrate adherence to security controls that govern machine identity usage.

Automated identity governance solutions enable organizations to meet compliance requirements by enforcing policy-driven controls for machine identity issuance, renewal, and revocation. Identity orchestration platforms integrate with cloud IAM services, certificate authorities, and secrets management tools to ensure that machine identities follow standardized security policies. Automated compliance reporting generates audit logs that document identity-related activities, access requests, and authentication events, providing organizations with the visibility needed to demonstrate regulatory adherence. By leveraging automated governance frameworks, enterprises can streamline compliance processes, reduce administrative overhead, and mitigate risks associated with manual identity management.

Machine identity monitoring and logging are essential for ensuring compliance with security standards and regulatory requirements. Organizations must implement centralized logging solutions that capture authentication attempts, failed login events, and identity-related access requests. Security information and event management (SIEM) platforms aggregate machine identity logs, enabling real-time analysis of identity usage and potential security threats. Compliance frameworks often require organizations to retain audit logs for extended periods, ensuring that identity activity records can be reviewed in the event of a security investigation. Implementing continuous monitoring and automated alerting helps organizations detect compliance violations, unauthorized access attempts, and potential identity compromises before they escalate into major security incidents.

Access control policies must align with regulatory standards to ensure that machine identities operate within the principle of least privilege. Role-based access control (RBAC) and attribute-based access control (ABAC) frameworks enforce fine-grained identity permissions, restricting machine identities from accessing resources beyond their intended scope. Compliance frameworks require organizations to conduct periodic access reviews, ensuring that machine identities do not accumulate excessive privileges over time. Automated access control enforcement prevents privilege escalation attacks, reducing the risk of unauthorized identity usage and regulatory non-compliance.

Regular security audits and compliance assessments help organizations evaluate their machine identity management practices and address potential gaps. Internal audits review identity issuance processes, certificate renewal policies, and API authentication mechanisms to ensure they align with regulatory mandates. External audits conducted by compliance certification bodies validate that organizations adhere to industry security standards, ensuring that machine identities are properly secured and monitored. By conducting regular security assessments, enterprises can proactively identify areas for improvement, remediate vulnerabilities, and strengthen their compliance posture.

Incident response and remediation are key components of regulatory compliance, ensuring that organizations can respond effectively to machine identity breaches. Compliance frameworks require organizations to have predefined incident response plans that outline procedures for detecting, containing, and mitigating identity-related security incidents. Automated incident response solutions integrate with identity management platforms, enabling rapid credential revocation, access restriction, and forensic investigation. Compliance-driven incident response strategies help organizations minimize the impact of machine identity breaches, maintain regulatory adherence, and demonstrate due diligence in security management.

Organizations must continuously adapt to evolving regulatory requirements and security best practices to ensure ongoing compliance with machine identity management standards. Emerging regulations, such as the European Union's Digital Operational Resilience Act (DORA) and the Cybersecurity Maturity Model Certification (CMMC), introduce additional security controls for protecting machine identities in financial services, defense, and critical infrastructure sectors. Organizations must stay informed of regulatory updates, implement adaptive security measures, and integrate compliance automation tools to maintain adherence to industry standards.

By implementing strong authentication mechanisms, enforcing access controls, conducting regular audits, and integrating automated governance frameworks, organizations can ensure compliance with regulatory requirements while mitigating risks associated with machine identity mismanagement. Regulatory standards provide a structured approach to securing machine identities, helping enterprises protect sensitive data, prevent unauthorized access, and maintain trust in digital interactions. As regulatory landscapes continue to evolve, organizations that prioritize compliance-driven machine identity management will be better equipped to navigate security challenges and maintain operational resilience in an increasingly complex digital environment.

Machine Identity Management in Financial Services

The financial services industry is one of the most targeted sectors for cyberattacks due to the high volume of sensitive transactions, personally identifiable information (PII), and regulatory obligations that govern banking and payment systems. As financial institutions transition to cloud-based infrastructure, digital banking, and automated financial transactions, the reliance on machine identities has grown exponentially. Machine identities—including API keys, digital certificates, cryptographic keys, and service accounts—play a fundamental role in securing transactions, authenticating services, and preventing fraud. However, the increasing complexity of financial ecosystems has also introduced significant security risks, making machine identity management a top priority for banks, payment processors, and investment firms.

Financial institutions use machine identities to secure a variety of critical services, including online banking platforms, mobile payment gateways, automated trading systems, and interbank communication networks. These identities authenticate transactions, establish encrypted communication channels, and enforce access controls to protect customer data from unauthorized access. Without proper machine identity management, financial organizations risk identity theft, credential misuse, insider threats, and compliance violations. A single compromised machine identity can enable attackers to impersonate trusted financial systems, bypass authentication controls, and gain unauthorized access to sensitive assets.

One of the key challenges in machine identity management for financial services is securing API-driven transactions. Banks and fintech companies increasingly rely on APIs to facilitate secure communication between mobile banking applications, third-party payment providers, and financial data aggregators. Open banking regulations such as PSD2 (Payment Services Directive 2) in Europe mandate that banks provide API access to authorized third-party providers, enabling consumers to share their financial data securely. However, improper API identity management can expose sensitive financial information to unauthorized entities, leading to data breaches and fraud. Strong authentication mechanisms, such as OAuth 2.0 and mutual TLS (mTLS), help ensure that only verified APIs can access financial data and execute transactions securely.

Digital certificates play a critical role in machine identity security by enabling encrypted communication between financial systems, cloud services, and customer-facing applications. Financial institutions use public key infrastructure (PKI) to issue and manage digital certificates, ensuring that all transactions are encrypted and authenticated. However, managing thousands of digital certificates across banking systems, payment networks, and trading platforms is a complex task.

Expired, misconfigured, or compromised certificates can lead to service outages, authentication failures, and security vulnerabilities. Automated certificate lifecycle management ensures that certificates are issued, renewed, and revoked dynamically, preventing operational disruptions and security risks associated with expired credentials.

Cryptographic key management is another essential component of machine identity security in financial services. Banks use encryption keys to protect financial transactions, digital signatures, and secure messaging protocols such as SWIFT (Society for Worldwide Interbank Financial Telecommunication). Improperly managed cryptographic keys pose significant risks, as compromised keys can be exploited to decrypt financial communications, forge transaction signatures, or manipulate account balances. Hardware security modules (HSMs) and key management services (KMS) provide secure storage and controlled access to cryptographic keys, ensuring that financial institutions maintain compliance with regulatory frameworks such as PCI-DSS (Payment Card Industry Data Security Standard) and NIST (National Institute of Standards and Technology).

Privileged access management (PAM) plays a crucial role in controlling machine identities with elevated permissions. Financial institutions must enforce strict access controls on machine identities used for high-risk operations, such as processing wire transfers, managing treasury accounts, and executing automated trading strategies. Role-based access control (RBAC) and attribute-based access control (ABAC) frameworks help limit the privileges assigned to machine identities, ensuring that only authorized systems can perform sensitive transactions. Just-in-time (JIT) access policies further enhance security by granting temporary machine identity credentials that expire automatically after use, reducing the risk of unauthorized access and insider threats.

Fraud detection and threat monitoring rely heavily on machine identity analytics to identify suspicious activity in real time. Financial organizations deploy advanced fraud detection systems that analyze machine identity behavior, transaction patterns, and authentication requests to detect anomalies. AI-driven machine learning models can identify deviations from normal transaction behavior, such as unauthorized API calls, excessive login attempts, or anomalous fund transfers. Integrating identity monitoring with security information and event management (SIEM) platforms enables financial institutions to detect identity misuse, revoke compromised credentials, and prevent fraudulent transactions before they impact customers.

Regulatory compliance is a key driver for machine identity management in financial services, as banks and financial institutions are subject to strict security mandates to protect customer data and transaction integrity. Regulations such as GDPR, SOX (Sarbanes-Oxley Act), and Basel III require financial organizations to implement strong identity governance, encryption standards, and access control mechanisms. Compliance frameworks mandate that financial institutions maintain audit logs of machine identity usage, monitor authentication events, and enforce policy-driven security controls. Non-compliance with regulatory standards can result in severe financial penalties, reputational damage, and legal consequences.

Zero trust security principles are increasingly being adopted in financial services to enhance machine identity protection. Under a zero trust model, machine identities are continuously verified based on contextual risk assessments before being granted access to financial systems. Conditional access policies evaluate multiple factors, including transaction value, geographic location, device security posture, and behavioral analytics, to determine whether a machine identity request should be approved or denied. By implementing zero trust authentication for machine identities, financial institutions can prevent identity spoofing, reduce attack surfaces, and mitigate advanced persistent threats (APTs).

Machine identity automation is essential for ensuring security at scale in financial services. As digital banking platforms, fintech applications, and cloud-native infrastructure expand, managing thousands or even millions of machine identities manually becomes impractical. Identity orchestration solutions integrate with cloud IAM platforms, certificate authorities, and secrets management tools to enforce standardized machine identity policies across multi-cloud and on-premises environments. Automating machine identity lifecycle management helps financial organizations reduce security risks, eliminate human errors, and maintain compliance with evolving regulatory requirements.

Incident response and recovery planning must include machine identity security to minimize the impact of identity-related breaches in financial institutions. Security teams must establish predefined response protocols for revoking compromised machine identities, rotating cryptographic keys, and isolating affected systems. Automated incident response workflows enable financial institutions to detect and contain identity-based threats rapidly, preventing attackers from exploiting stolen credentials to commit financial fraud or disrupt banking operations. Conducting regular penetration testing and red teaming exercises helps organizations validate their incident response readiness and strengthen their machine identity security posture.

As financial services continue to evolve with digital transformation, machine identity management will remain a cornerstone of security, compliance, and fraud prevention. By implementing robust authentication mechanisms, enforcing strict access controls, automating certificate and key management, and integrating real-time threat detection, financial institutions can protect their critical assets, maintain regulatory compliance, and build customer trust in an increasingly interconnected financial ecosystem. Organizations that prioritize machine identity security will be better positioned to defend against emerging cyber threats and maintain the integrity of digital financial transactions.

Healthcare and Medical Device Identity Security

The healthcare industry is undergoing rapid digital transformation, integrating cloud-based services, electronic health records (EHRs), telemedicine platforms, and connected medical devices to improve patient care and operational efficiency. These advancements rely on machine identities to enable secure communication between systems, authenticate medical devices, and protect sensitive patient data. However, the increasing use of interconnected medical devices and cloud-based healthcare applications has also introduced new cybersecurity challenges. Machine identity security is critical for protecting healthcare infrastructure, preventing unauthorized access, and ensuring compliance with stringent regulatory frameworks.

Medical devices, including infusion pumps, heart monitors, imaging systems, and ventilators, generate and transmit sensitive patient data across hospital networks. These devices rely on machine identities, such as digital certificates, API tokens, and cryptographic keys, to authenticate themselves, establish secure communication channels, and integrate with EHR systems. However, many legacy medical devices were not designed with strong security measures, making them vulnerable to identity spoofing, unauthorized access, and cyberattacks. If an attacker compromises a machine identity, they can manipulate medical device functionality, alter patient records, or disrupt critical healthcare services.

The use of machine identities extends beyond medical devices to cloud-based healthcare platforms, where applications, APIs, and automated workflows require authentication to access patient information and medical imaging data. Telemedicine platforms, mobile health apps, and remote patient monitoring systems rely on API-driven interactions between cloud services and on-premises healthcare systems. Without proper identity security, attackers can exploit exposed API keys, intercept sensitive patient data, or gain control over cloud-based medical services. Strong authentication mechanisms, such as mutual TLS (mTLS), OAuth 2.0, and certificate-based authentication, are necessary to verify the legitimacy of machine identities before granting access to healthcare systems.

Regulatory compliance mandates strict security controls for managing machine identities in healthcare environments. The Health Insurance Portability and Accountability Act (HIPAA) in the United States requires healthcare organizations to implement strong authentication, encryption, and access control measures to protect electronic protected health information (ePHI). The General Data Protection Regulation (GDPR) in the European Union enforces similar requirements for securing personal health data. Compliance with these regulations requires healthcare organizations to maintain audit logs of machine identity usage, enforce least privilege access policies, and implement security measures that prevent unauthorized access to patient records.

Certificate-based authentication plays a crucial role in securing machine identities in healthcare. Digital certificates enable encrypted communication between medical devices, hospital networks, and cloud-based services, ensuring that sensitive data remains confidential during transmission. However, managing digital certificates across a complex healthcare environment is challenging, as expired or misconfigured certificates can disrupt medical services. Automated certificate lifecycle management ensures that certificates are issued, renewed, and revoked in real time, preventing service outages and security gaps associated with expired credentials.

Medical device manufacturers must prioritize machine identity security during the design and development of new devices. Many legacy medical devices lack modern security features, making them easy targets for cyberattacks. Secure boot mechanisms, cryptographic identity verification, and embedded hardware security modules (HSMs) help protect medical devices from identity spoofing and unauthorized firmware modifications. Device identity attestation ensures that only trusted medical devices can connect to hospital networks and access patient data. Manufacturers must integrate machine identity security into the entire product lifecycle, from initial deployment to ongoing software updates and patch management.

Access control policies are essential for restricting machine identity privileges within healthcare environments. Role-based access control (RBAC) and attribute-based access control (ABAC) frameworks define which medical devices, applications, and services can access specific healthcare resources. For example, an infusion pump should only have permissions to communicate with the hospital pharmacy system to retrieve medication dosage information, but it should not have access to patient financial records. Implementing strict access policies prevents overprivileged machine identities from being exploited for unauthorized activities.

Monitoring and anomaly detection help identify compromised machine identities before they are used for malicious purposes. Healthcare organizations must continuously track authentication events, device interactions, and API usage to detect suspicious activity. Anomalous behavior, such as a medical device attempting to access unauthorized systems or excessive API requests from a cloud-based healthcare platform, may indicate a security breach. Security information and event management (SIEM) platforms aggregate identity-related logs, allowing security teams to investigate and respond to potential threats in real time.

Cryptographic key management is another crucial aspect of machine identity security in healthcare. Encryption keys protect sensitive medical data, secure communication channels, and verify the authenticity of medical devices. However, if encryption keys are not managed properly, they can be compromised or misused. Healthcare organizations must use key management solutions (KMS) to store, rotate, and enforce access controls on cryptographic keys. Hardware security modules (HSMs) provide an additional layer of protection by isolating encryption operations from unauthorized access.

The adoption of zero trust security models strengthens machine identity security in healthcare environments. Under a zero trust framework, machine identities are continuously authenticated and authorized before being granted access to hospital networks, cloud platforms, and patient data repositories. Conditional access policies evaluate factors such as device security posture, network location, and historical identity behavior to determine whether a machine identity request should be approved. Implementing zero trust security for machine identities helps prevent unauthorized access, identity spoofing, and lateral movement within healthcare networks.

Incident response and recovery planning must account for machine identity breaches in healthcare settings. If a medical device identity is compromised, security teams must quickly revoke its credentials, isolate the affected device, and investigate potential data breaches. Automated incident response workflows enable healthcare organizations to disable compromised machine identities, rotate encryption keys, and restore secure access to critical medical systems. Conducting regular penetration testing and security assessments helps identify vulnerabilities in machine identity management processes and improve incident response readiness.

Interoperability between healthcare systems further complicates machine identity security. Hospitals, clinics, and insurance providers rely on interconnected networks and shared data repositories, requiring machine identities to authenticate across multiple systems. Standardized identity federation protocols, such as SAML (Security Assertion Markup Language) and OAuth, facilitate secure authentication between different healthcare entities. However, improperly configured federated identities can introduce security risks if not properly managed. Healthcare organizations must enforce strict identity governance policies to ensure that machine identities maintain integrity across interconnected healthcare ecosystems.

Healthcare supply chain security is another critical area where machine identity management plays a role. Medical devices, pharmaceutical supply chains, and hospital IT infrastructure depend on machine identities to authenticate suppliers, manufacturers, and distributors. Attackers targeting the healthcare supply chain can exploit misconfigured machine identities to introduce counterfeit medical products, manipulate device firmware, or disrupt logistics operations. Strong identity verification, digital signatures, and blockchain-based authentication mechanisms help secure the healthcare supply chain and prevent identity fraud.

As healthcare technology continues to evolve, machine identity security will remain a top priority for protecting patient data, ensuring medical device integrity, and maintaining regulatory compliance. By implementing automated certificate management, enforcing access control policies, integrating real-time monitoring, and adopting zero trust security models, healthcare organizations can safeguard machine identities against cyber threats and unauthorized access. A proactive approach to machine identity management enables healthcare providers to deliver secure, reliable, and resilient medical services while maintaining trust in an increasingly connected healthcare ecosystem.

Government and Defense: Machine Identity Challenges

Government and defense organizations operate in some of the most complex and high-risk cybersecurity environments, requiring robust security frameworks to protect sensitive data, national security assets, and critical infrastructure. As governments increasingly digitize their operations, the number of machine identities in use has surged, encompassing everything from secure communication networks and defense systems to intelligence platforms and classified databases. Machine identities—such as cryptographic keys, digital certificates, API tokens, and service accounts—are essential for securing government systems, enabling authentication, encryption, and access control for both internal and external communications. However, the growing reliance on machine identities presents significant security challenges, including identity sprawl, nation-state cyber threats, supply chain risks, and the complexities of maintaining secure identity management across classified and unclassified networks.

One of the primary challenges in government and defense environments is managing the scale and complexity of machine identities. Unlike commercial enterprises, which typically operate within defined regulatory frameworks, government agencies must secure identities across highly fragmented and interconnected ecosystems. These ecosystems include military networks, law enforcement databases, intelligence agencies, cloud infrastructure, and international partnerships. Each entity within this ecosystem relies on machine identities to verify trust, but improper identity governance can lead to misconfigurations, unauthorized access, and security gaps that adversaries can exploit. The challenge is exacerbated by the rapid expansion of cloud-based government services, edge computing in defense operations, and Internet of Things (IoT) devices used in surveillance, border security, and emergency response systems.

Nation-state cyber threats pose a significant risk to government machine identities, as state-sponsored actors continuously target authentication mechanisms, cryptographic credentials, and secure communication channels. These adversaries use advanced persistent threats (APTs) to infiltrate government networks, steal classified information, and disrupt critical systems. Compromised machine identities provide attackers with an entry point to impersonate trusted services, intercept encrypted government communications, and conduct cyber espionage campaigns. Protecting machine identities against nation-state attacks requires strong authentication protocols, continuous identity monitoring, and the implementation of zero trust security models to prevent unauthorized access.

The integration of machine identities into military and defense systems introduces additional security risks, particularly in securing autonomous weapon systems, defense satellites, and battlefield communications. Military-grade encryption is essential for ensuring that machine identities used in defense applications remain protected against adversaries attempting to intercept, manipulate, or disable mission-critical systems. Tactical networks, which rely on machine identities to authenticate encrypted communication between command centers and deployed forces, must be secured against identity spoofing and unauthorized access attempts. Defense agencies must enforce strict cryptographic policies, leveraging hardware security modules (HSMs) and quantum-resistant encryption algorithms to protect machine identities in high-risk environments.

Supply chain security is another major challenge in machine identity management for government and defense organizations. Many government agencies rely on third-party contractors, technology vendors, and international suppliers to develop and maintain critical infrastructure. However, compromised machine identities within the supply chain can serve as backdoors for attackers to introduce vulnerabilities, inject malicious code, or impersonate legitimate systems. The SolarWinds cyberattack, for example, demonstrated how attackers exploited supply chain vulnerabilities by compromising software updates, using machine identities to distribute malware across multiple government agencies. Strengthening supply chain security requires enforcing strict identity verification for third-party entities, implementing cryptographic signing for software components, and continuously monitoring identity behaviors within government networks.

The increasing use of cloud-based government services has introduced new challenges in securing machine identities across hybrid and multi-cloud environments. While cloud platforms offer scalability and efficiency, they also expand the attack surface for cyber threats targeting machine identities. Government agencies must ensure that machine identities used in cloud-based applications are properly managed, with automated certificate lifecycle management, just-in-time (JIT) credential provisioning, and strict access control policies. Cloud security frameworks such as FedRAMP (Federal Risk and Authorization Management Program) establish compliance requirements for securing machine identities in government cloud environments, but agencies must also implement continuous monitoring to detect unauthorized identity use or misconfigurations that could expose sensitive data.

The implementation of zero trust security models is critical for addressing machine identity challenges in government and defense operations. Unlike traditional perimeter-based security models, zero trust frameworks assume that no machine identity should be inherently trusted, regardless of whether it originates from inside or outside a government network. Under zero trust principles, machine identities are continuously authenticated and authorized based on real-time risk assessments, ensuring that access to government resources is granted only after verifying multiple security factors. Micro-segmentation further enhances zero trust by limiting machine identity privileges to specific systems, preventing lateral movement if an identity is compromised.

Machine identity automation is essential for managing the vast number of credentials, certificates, and authentication tokens used across government and defense networks. Manually provisioning and revoking machine identities at scale is impractical, leading to identity sprawl and potential security gaps. Automated identity governance solutions integrate with public key infrastructure (PKI), certificate authorities (CAs), and identity and access management (IAM) frameworks to enforce consistent security policies. By automating certificate issuance, key rotation, and identity revocation, government agencies can reduce administrative overhead while ensuring that machine identities remain secure and compliant with regulatory requirements.

The challenge of balancing security with operational continuity is particularly relevant in defense and intelligence operations, where secure machine identities must be maintained even in highly dynamic environments. Military operations, for example, require secure machine identities that can function reliably in disconnected or contested networks where centralized identity management may not be feasible. Tactical identity authentication solutions, such as air-gapped identity verification, cryptographic time-stamping, and blockchain-based identity registries, help ensure that machine identities remain verifiable and tamper-proof even in adversarial conditions.

Incident response and threat intelligence integration play a vital role in mitigating machine identity threats in government and defense environments. Security teams must have real-time visibility into machine identity activity, enabling them to detect and respond to unauthorized identity use, credential misuse, and suspected cyber espionage attempts. Threat intelligence platforms provide insights into emerging attack tactics, helping government agencies proactively adjust their identity security policies. Automated incident response workflows allow agencies to revoke compromised machine identities, block malicious authentication attempts, and isolate affected systems without disrupting critical operations.

Regulatory compliance mandates that government agencies enforce strict identity governance policies, ensuring that machine identities adhere to security standards such as NIST 800-53, ISO 27001, and CJIS (Criminal Justice Information Services) security policies. These regulations require government entities to implement encryption, access controls, audit logging, and incident response measures to protect sensitive data and national security assets. Compliance-driven machine identity management ensures that agencies maintain accountability while reducing the risk of identity-based cyberattacks.

As government and defense organizations continue to adopt digital transformation initiatives, securing machine identities will remain a top priority for protecting classified data, securing national infrastructure, and defending against state-sponsored cyber threats. By implementing zero trust authentication, automating identity governance, securing cloud environments, and strengthening supply chain protections, government agencies can enhance their resilience against machine identity compromises. The future of national security depends on the ability to protect machine identities in an evolving cyber threat landscape, ensuring that critical systems, defense operations, and government services remain secure from adversaries seeking to exploit identity vulnerabilities.

Telecommunications and Machine Identity Risks

The telecommunications industry serves as the backbone of global communication, enabling billions of people and devices to connect across networks, data centers, and cloud environments. As telecom providers expand their services to include 5G, IoT connectivity, and edge computing, the number of machine identities in use has grown exponentially. These identities, which include digital certificates, API keys, SIM card credentials, and cryptographic tokens, play a critical role in securing data transmission, authenticating network devices, and enabling automated service provisioning. However, the increasing reliance on machine identities has introduced new cybersecurity risks that threaten the integrity of telecommunications networks and expose providers to identity-based attacks.

One of the biggest risks in telecommunications is the compromise of machine identities used in network infrastructure. Telecom providers operate vast networks that include core systems, mobile towers, fiber optic connections, and software-defined networking (SDN) controllers. Each of these components requires a secure machine identity to authenticate itself and communicate securely with other network elements. If an attacker gains access to a compromised machine identity, they can infiltrate the telecom infrastructure, intercept sensitive communications, and manipulate network traffic. Cybercriminals and state-sponsored threat actors target machine identities to conduct man-in-the-middle (MITM) attacks, allowing them to eavesdrop on private conversations, inject malicious payloads, or disrupt telecom services.

5G networks introduce additional machine identity risks due to their highly dynamic and software-driven architecture. Unlike previous generations of mobile networks, 5G relies on virtualization, network slicing, and distributed edge computing, creating an explosion of machine-to-machine authentication requests. Each connected device, from smartphones to industrial IoT sensors, requires a unique machine identity to establish secure connections with the network. Telecom operators must ensure that digital certificates and authentication tokens used in 5G networks are properly managed, rotated, and revoked to prevent unauthorized access and service disruptions. Weak identity security in 5G environments can lead to SIM cloning attacks, identity spoofing, and unauthorized access to critical network functions.

Machine identity mismanagement also presents a risk to API security in telecommunications. Telecom providers expose APIs to enable interoperability between network functions, third-party applications, and cloud services. These APIs allow mobile carriers to integrate billing systems, roaming services, and customer management platforms. However, if API keys and authentication tokens are not properly secured, attackers can exploit them to gain unauthorized access to telecom infrastructure, extract subscriber data, or disrupt service availability. API abuse is a growing threat in the telecom sector, with attackers using stolen machine identities to conduct fraud, bypass network controls, and launch denial-of-service (DoS) attacks.

IoT device proliferation further complicates machine identity management in telecom networks. The deployment of billions of IoT devices, including smart meters, connected vehicles, and industrial sensors, requires telecom providers to authenticate and manage an unprecedented number of machine identities. Many IoT devices rely on weak authentication mechanisms, such as default credentials or static encryption keys, making them easy targets for cyberattacks. If an attacker compromises the identity of an IoT device, they can use it to gain access to telecom networks, spread malware, or disrupt critical services. Implementing strong identity verification, device attestation, and automated certificate management is essential for mitigating IoT-related identity risks.

Telecom providers also face risks associated with machine identity lifecycle management. Expired or misconfigured digital certificates can lead to service outages, failed authentication requests, and security vulnerabilities. Many telecom operators use public key infrastructure (PKI) to issue and manage digital certificates for network components, but manual certificate management processes are prone to errors. If a critical certificate expires without renewal, it can disrupt secure connections between network nodes, leading to dropped calls, degraded internet performance, or loss of service availability. Automated certificate lifecycle management helps telecom providers ensure that machine identities remain valid and secure throughout their operational lifespan.

Another growing concern in telecommunications is insider threats targeting machine identities. Employees, contractors, and third-party vendors with access to network infrastructure may misuse machine identities for malicious purposes. Insider threats can involve credential theft, unauthorized configuration changes, or deliberate service disruptions. Weak access controls and overprivileged machine identities increase the risk of insider-related security incidents. Telecom operators must enforce strict role-based access control (RBAC) and attribute-based access control (ABAC) policies to limit machine identity permissions based on operational needs. Just-in-time (JIT) access policies further reduce insider threats by granting temporary credentials that expire after predefined periods.

Supply chain vulnerabilities add another layer of risk to machine identity security in telecommunications. Telecom providers depend on a global supply chain for network equipment, software components, and cloud services. If a supplier's machine identity is compromised, attackers can introduce backdoors, tamper with software updates, or install rogue network components that enable long-term espionage. Recent cyberattacks on telecom vendors have highlighted the risks of compromised firmware, hardware implants, and counterfeit certificates being used to infiltrate telecom networks. Strengthening supply chain security requires telecom operators to enforce strict identity verification for third-party providers, conduct continuous security audits, and implement cryptographic signing for all software and firmware updates.

Regulatory compliance plays a crucial role in shaping machine identity security in telecommunications. Governments and regulatory bodies impose strict security standards to ensure telecom networks remain resilient against cyber threats. Regulations such as the EU's General Data Protection Regulation (GDPR), the U.S. Federal Communications Commission (FCC) cybersecurity guidelines, and the Telecommunication Security Act (TSA) require telecom providers to implement strong authentication, encryption, and identity governance controls. Compliance mandates also require telecom operators to maintain audit logs of machine identity activity, monitor access requests, and report security incidents involving compromised identities.

To mitigate machine identity risks, telecom providers must implement a zero trust security framework that continuously verifies machine identities before granting network access. Zero trust principles dictate that no machine identity should be inherently trusted, and access should be granted based on real-time risk assessments. Multi-factor authentication (MFA), continuous identity monitoring, and network segmentation help enforce zero trust security for telecom networks. By dynamically adjusting machine identity permissions based on security conditions, telecom providers can reduce attack surfaces and prevent unauthorized access to critical infrastructure.

Threat intelligence integration further strengthens machine identity security in telecommunications. Telecom providers must leverage global threat intelligence feeds to identify known attack patterns, detect compromised machine identities, and block malicious authentication attempts in real time. Advanced threat detection systems use machine learning to analyze identity-related anomalies, flagging suspicious activities such as credential stuffing, unauthorized API usage, and machine identity spoofing. By proactively identifying identity threats, telecom operators can respond to cyberattacks before they escalate into major network disruptions.

Incident response planning is critical for mitigating machine identity breaches in telecom networks. When a machine identity is compromised, telecom providers must act swiftly to revoke credentials, isolate affected systems, and restore secure communication channels. Automated incident response workflows help security teams contain threats by rotating compromised keys, enforcing access restrictions, and deploying forensic analysis tools to assess the extent of the breach. Regular security drills, red teaming exercises, and penetration testing ensure that telecom operators remain prepared to handle machine identity incidents effectively.

As telecommunications networks continue to expand with 5G, IoT, and cloud-based services, securing machine identities must remain a top priority. By implementing automated identity lifecycle management, enforcing strict access controls, adopting zero trust principles, and integrating real-time threat detection, telecom providers can protect their infrastructure from identity-related cyber threats. A proactive approach to machine identity security ensures the reliability, resilience, and security of global communication networks in an increasingly digital world.

Future Trends in Machine Identity Management

As enterprises continue to expand their digital ecosystems, machine identity management is becoming increasingly complex and critical for cybersecurity. The number of machine identities is growing exponentially, driven by the proliferation of cloud computing, the rise of Internet of Things (IoT) devices, the expansion of artificial intelligence (AI)-driven automation, and the adoption of decentralized applications. Traditional identity and access management (IAM) approaches are no longer sufficient to manage the vast number of machine identities interacting within these environments. Emerging trends in machine identity management focus on automation, enhanced cryptographic protections, artificial intelligence integration, zero trust security models, and the use of decentralized identity frameworks.

The automation of machine identity lifecycle management is becoming a necessity as organizations struggle to keep up with the scale and complexity of their machine identities. Managing certificates, API keys, cryptographic tokens, and service accounts manually is no longer feasible, especially in multi-cloud environments where workloads and microservices spin up and down dynamically. Future advancements in machine identity management will focus on identity orchestration platforms that provide centralized policy enforcement, automated certificate issuance and renewal, and just-in-time (JIT) credential provisioning. These automation capabilities will reduce the risk of human error, prevent expired credentials from disrupting operations, and ensure that machine identities comply with security policies in real time.

Quantum computing presents both opportunities and challenges for machine identity security. Current encryption algorithms used in machine identities rely on public key cryptography, which could become vulnerable once quantum computers reach a sufficient level of computational power. Cryptographic techniques such as RSA and ECC (Elliptic Curve Cryptography) may no longer be secure against quantum attacks, leading to the need for quantum-resistant cryptographic algorithms. Governments and enterprises are already researching post-quantum cryptography (PQC) solutions, which will play a critical role in the future of machine identity management. Organizations will need to transition their machine identities to quantum-safe encryption methods, ensuring that their authentication mechanisms remain secure in a post-quantum world.

Artificial intelligence and machine learning are set to transform machine identity management by enabling predictive security analytics and automated threat detection. AI-driven security tools will analyze vast amounts of machine identity telemetry data to detect anomalies, flag unauthorized identity usage, and automatically revoke compromised credentials. Machine learning models will continuously learn from authentication patterns, allowing security systems to differentiate between normal identity behavior and potential threats in real time. AI will also enhance risk-based authentication, dynamically adjusting machine identity permissions based on contextual signals such as location, behavior, and historical access patterns.

Zero trust security models will play an even greater role in machine identity management, enforcing continuous authentication and authorization for all machine-to-machine interactions. The traditional perimeter-based security approach is no longer effective in protecting dynamic cloud environments, containerized workloads, and distributed IoT networks. Zero trust frameworks require that every machine identity be verified at every access request, regardless of whether it originates from inside or outside the enterprise network. This means that machine identities will need to be continuously validated based on risk scores, threat intelligence feeds, and behavioral analytics, reducing the chances of unauthorized access through compromised credentials.

Decentralized identity frameworks are emerging as an alternative to traditional machine identity management approaches. Technologies such as blockchain and distributed ledger systems enable machine identities to be independently verified without relying on centralized certificate authorities (CAs) or identity providers (IdPs). In a decentralized identity model, each machine identity is cryptographically secured within a distributed ledger, providing a tamper-proof record of authentication events. This approach reduces reliance on single points of failure and enhances identity trust in environments where multiple entities need to authenticate securely without exposing sensitive credentials. As decentralized identity solutions mature, they may become a standard approach for managing machine identities in financial services, government systems, and IoT networks.

The integration of machine identity management with cloud-native security solutions is another key trend shaping the future of identity governance. Cloud service providers are increasingly embedding machine identity management capabilities into their security frameworks, enabling seamless identity lifecycle automation across hybrid and multi-cloud environments. Organizations will move toward identity-aware networking, where machine identities are integrated directly into software-defined networking (SDN) and cloud-native security controls. This will allow for more granular identity-based access control, preventing lateral movement attacks and ensuring that only authenticated workloads can communicate with each other.

Federated machine identity management is also gaining traction, allowing organizations to securely share machine identities across different entities, business partners, and service providers. Just as federated identity solutions enable seamless authentication for human users across multiple organizations, federated machine identity frameworks will allow different enterprises to verify and authenticate machine identities without exposing raw credentials. This will be particularly important for securing interconnected supply chains, where manufacturers, logistics providers, and distributors need to authenticate machine-to-machine communications securely without relying on traditional IAM mechanisms.

The rise of edge computing and 5G networks is driving the need for machine identity management at the network edge. As organizations deploy distributed edge computing nodes, mobile network towers, and real-time analytics systems, the number of machine identities required to authenticate these components is increasing dramatically. Future advancements in machine identity security will focus on lightweight identity verification mechanisms that can operate efficiently on edge devices with limited computing resources. Cryptographic attestation, hardware-based identity verification, and secure enclaves will become essential technologies for ensuring that machine identities remain protected at the edge.

Compliance and regulatory requirements will continue to evolve, placing greater emphasis on machine identity governance. Governments and regulatory bodies are expected to introduce stricter identity verification standards to prevent identity fraud, data breaches, and unauthorized machine-to-machine interactions. Organizations will need to adopt continuous compliance monitoring tools that automatically assess machine identity security postures, generate audit logs, and enforce policy-driven remediation workflows. AI-powered compliance automation will play a crucial role in helping organizations meet regulatory mandates by identifying security gaps and ensuring that machine identities remain in compliance with industry standards.

The future of machine identity management will also focus on enhancing interoperability between different security frameworks. With organizations using a mix of cloud providers, on-premises systems, IoT devices, and SaaS applications, managing machine identities across heterogeneous environments remains a challenge. Future solutions will emphasize open identity standards, cross-platform integration, and identity interoperability to ensure seamless authentication across diverse IT ecosystems. Standardized identity protocols such as OAuth 2.1, FIDO2, and decentralized identity standards will help bridge identity management gaps between different technology stacks.

As cyber threats targeting machine identities continue to evolve, organizations will need to stay ahead of attackers by implementing proactive security measures, embracing automation, and adopting emerging identity management technologies. The future of machine identity management will be defined by greater intelligence, automation, and adaptability, ensuring that organizations can securely authenticate and manage machine identities in an increasingly interconnected digital world.

Quantum Computing and the Future of Machine Identity Security

Quantum computing represents a revolutionary advancement in computational power, capable of solving complex problems at speeds unattainable by classical computers. While quantum technology has the potential to drive innovation across multiple industries, it also introduces significant security concerns, particularly in the realm of machine identity management. The cryptographic foundations that secure digital certificates, authentication mechanisms, and encryption protocols are at risk of becoming obsolete once quantum computers reach a sufficient level of computational maturity. The future of machine identity security depends on the transition to quantum-resistant cryptographic techniques, the development of new identity verification frameworks, and the ability to defend against quantum-enabled cyber threats.

Machine identities, including digital certificates, API keys, cryptographic tokens, and service accounts, rely on public key infrastructure (PKI) to establish trust and enable secure communication. Current PKI implementations use asymmetric cryptographic algorithms such as RSA (Rivest-Shamir-Adleman), ECC (Elliptic Curve Cryptography), and DSA (Digital Signature Algorithm) to generate machine identities, authenticate services, and encrypt data transmissions. These encryption techniques rely on the computational difficulty of factoring large prime numbers or solving discrete logarithm problems, which are practically impossible for classical computers to break within a reasonable timeframe. However, quantum computers introduce a new paradigm where these encryption methods could become vulnerable to rapid decryption using quantum algorithms.

Shor's algorithm, developed by mathematician Peter Shor, is one of the most concerning quantum advancements for cryptography. It enables quantum computers to factor large prime numbers exponentially faster than classical methods, effectively rendering RSA and ECC encryption schemes insecure. If a sufficiently powerful quantum computer is developed, machine identities that rely on these cryptographic techniques could be decrypted in minutes or even seconds. This poses a major risk to secure communications, data protection, and machine-to-machine authentication, as attackers could exploit quantum computing to forge digital certificates, impersonate trusted services, and decrypt sensitive data without detection.

The transition to quantum-resistant cryptographic algorithms, known as post-quantum cryptography (PQC), is a critical step in securing machine identities against quantum threats. Governments, research institutions, and cybersecurity organizations are actively developing and standardizing cryptographic techniques that can withstand quantum attacks. The National Institute of Standards and Technology (NIST) has been leading the effort to identify quantum-safe encryption algorithms through its Post-Quantum Cryptography Standardization Project. These new cryptographic schemes aim to replace vulnerable algorithms with lattice-based, multivariate, hash-based, and code-based encryption methods that are resistant to quantum decryption techniques.

One of the challenges in adopting post-quantum cryptography for machine identity security is the large-scale migration required across existing digital infrastructures. Enterprises, cloud providers, and security vendors must replace their current cryptographic implementations with quantum-safe alternatives while ensuring backward compatibility with legacy systems. Machine identity management platforms will need to support hybrid cryptographic models, where both classical and post-quantum algorithms coexist during the transition period. This hybrid approach allows organizations to gradually phase out vulnerable encryption methods while maintaining secure authentication and encryption protocols.

Quantum-safe PKI will play a crucial role in securing machine identities in the post-quantum era. Certificate authorities (CAs) must adapt their certificate issuance processes to incorporate quantum-resistant encryption methods, ensuring that digital certificates remain secure against future quantum attacks. Machine identities that rely on traditional PKI infrastructures will need to undergo cryptographic agility upgrades, allowing for seamless reissuance and renewal using quantum-safe algorithms. Organizations will also need to implement quantum-resistant key exchange mechanisms, such as lattice-based key encapsulation, to protect machine-to-machine communication from quantum-enabled interception.

Beyond cryptographic advancements, quantum computing also introduces new challenges in secure identity verification. Traditional identity authentication models, including multi-factor authentication (MFA) and token-based authentication, may require enhancements to withstand quantum attacks. Quantum-secure authentication techniques, such as zero-knowledge proofs (ZKPs) and quantum key distribution (QKD), provide promising solutions for ensuring that machine identities remain protected in a quantum-capable adversarial landscape. Zero-knowledge proofs enable identity verification without exposing sensitive information, reducing the risk of credential theft and impersonation attacks. Quantum key distribution leverages the principles of quantum mechanics to establish secure communication channels, preventing eavesdroppers from intercepting encryption keys during transmission.

The impact of quantum computing on machine identity security extends beyond encryption to broader cybersecurity concerns, including quantum-enabled cyberattacks. Quantum-powered machine learning models could be used by threat actors to analyze authentication patterns, predict encryption keys, and automate large-scale identity-based attacks. Attackers leveraging quantum computing resources may be able to bypass traditional anomaly detection systems, making it imperative for security teams to adopt quantum-resilient threat intelligence and monitoring solutions. Organizations must invest in AI-driven behavioral analytics to detect and mitigate identity misuse, ensuring that machine identities are not exploited through advanced quantum-based attack methodologies.

Governments and regulatory bodies are beginning to acknowledge the risks posed by quantum computing to cybersecurity. National security agencies and defense organizations are investing in quantum-resistant infrastructure to protect classified communications, critical infrastructure, and military assets from quantum-enabled adversaries. Compliance frameworks are expected to evolve, introducing new security mandates that require organizations to implement quantum-safe identity management practices. Enterprises operating in regulated industries, such as finance, healthcare, and telecommunications, will need to stay ahead of regulatory changes by adopting quantum-resistant identity security measures and demonstrating compliance with emerging cryptographic standards.

Preparing for the quantum future requires a proactive approach to machine identity security. Organizations must conduct comprehensive risk assessments to evaluate their exposure to quantum threats, identifying machine identities that rely on vulnerable encryption algorithms. Security teams should implement quantum-readiness roadmaps, outlining phased migration strategies for transitioning to post-quantum cryptographic standards. Vendor collaboration and industry-wide initiatives will be essential in ensuring a smooth transition, as enterprises work alongside security providers to adopt quantum-safe identity management solutions.

The evolution of machine identity security in the quantum era will demand continuous innovation, adaptability, and collaboration. Cybersecurity professionals must stay informed about quantum advancements, actively participating in cryptographic research and industry discussions. Organizations must embrace cryptographic agility, ensuring that their machine identity frameworks can adapt to emerging threats and quantum breakthroughs. As quantum computing progresses toward practical implementation, enterprises that invest in quantum-resilient identity management today will be better equipped to safeguard their digital infrastructure in the future.

Blockchain and Decentralized Machine Identities

The rise of blockchain technology has introduced new possibilities for securing and managing machine identities in decentralized and trustless environments. Traditional machine identity management relies on centralized authorities such as certificate authorities (CAs), identity providers (IdPs), and public key infrastructure (PKI) to issue and validate machine credentials. While these systems have served as the foundation for authentication and encryption, they introduce security risks, including single points of failure, certificate mismanagement, and unauthorized identity issuance. Blockchain-based decentralized identity frameworks offer an alternative approach that enhances security, removes central authority dependencies, and enables greater transparency in machine identity verification.

Decentralized machine identities leverage blockchain's distributed ledger technology (DLT) to provide tamper-proof, verifiable, and immutable identity records. Unlike traditional identity management systems, where a central authority issues and revokes machine identities, blockchain allows identities to be self-sovereign, meaning each entity maintains control over its own identity without relying on intermediaries. This is particularly beneficial in environments where multiple organizations, devices, or services need to authenticate each other without exposing sensitive credentials to third-party providers. Blockchain's cryptographic security mechanisms ensure that machine identities remain resistant to forgery, unauthorized modifications, and identity theft.

One of the core components of decentralized machine identity management is the use of decentralized identifiers (DIDs). DIDs are globally unique, cryptographically verifiable identifiers that are registered on a blockchain or distributed ledger rather than being issued by a central authority. Each DID is associated with a pair of cryptographic keys that allow machines to sign transactions, authenticate themselves, and establish trust in a peer-to-peer network. Since DIDs are not tied to a single entity, they provide a flexible and secure mechanism for verifying machine identities across different ecosystems, such as cloud environments, IoT networks, and financial services.

Smart contracts, another key feature of blockchain technology, play a critical role in decentralized machine identity management. Smart contracts are self-executing agreements encoded into blockchain networks that enforce identity verification rules without requiring manual intervention. When a machine identity requests access to a resource, a smart contract can validate the identity's credentials, enforce access policies, and record authentication events immutably on the blockchain. This automation reduces reliance on centralized identity providers, eliminates manual approval processes, and ensures that identity transactions remain transparent and auditable.

Blockchain-based identity management also enhances security by reducing the risk of certificate misuse and unauthorized credential issuance. Traditional PKI systems depend on trusted certificate authorities to issue and revoke digital certificates, but these CAs can be compromised, leading to fraudulent certificate issuance. Blockchain eliminates the need for centralized CAs by allowing machine identities to register their own cryptographic keys on a decentralized ledger. This means that even if a single entity is compromised, the integrity of the overall identity system remains intact. Organizations can verify the authenticity of machine identities in real time without needing to rely on third-party verification services.

The integration of blockchain with machine identity security has significant implications for IoT networks, where billions of connected devices require authentication and secure communication. Many IoT devices operate in distributed environments without stable network access, making traditional identity management approaches impractical. Blockchain provides a decentralized trust model that enables IoT devices to authenticate themselves securely without requiring a constant connection to a central server. By recording device identities, authentication events, and security updates on an immutable ledger, organizations can establish an auditable chain of trust that prevents identity spoofing, unauthorized access, and device tampering.

Decentralized machine identities also improve security in cloud and multi-cloud environments, where workloads frequently move across different providers. In traditional cloud identity management, each cloud service provider maintains its own identity framework, requiring organizations to manage multiple authentication mechanisms and identity federation processes. Blockchain-based identity management provides a unified, provider-agnostic approach, enabling machine identities to be verified across different cloud environments without relying on proprietary identity management systems. This reduces identity fragmentation, simplifies authentication workflows, and enhances interoperability between cloud providers.

Another advantage of decentralized identity management is the ability to implement self-sovereign identities for machines in industries such as financial services, healthcare, and telecommunications. In these sectors, machines must interact with multiple regulatory frameworks, third-party vendors, and supply chain partners, creating complex identity verification requirements. Blockchain enables organizations to establish verifiable credentials that can be independently validated by authorized entities without exposing raw identity data. For example, in the financial sector, a machine identity could present a verifiable credential proving its compliance with regulatory standards, without sharing sensitive cryptographic keys or internal security details.

Despite its advantages, blockchain-based machine identity management faces several challenges, including scalability, regulatory compliance, and integration with existing identity frameworks. Blockchain networks must handle large volumes of identity transactions efficiently while maintaining low latency for authentication requests. Permissioned blockchains, which restrict identity verification to approved entities, offer a potential solution by balancing decentralization with performance optimization. However, organizations must carefully evaluate the trade-offs between public, private, and consortium blockchains when implementing decentralized identity solutions.

Regulatory compliance is another consideration in blockchain-based machine identity management. Many industries require identity records to be maintained under strict data protection laws, such as GDPR, HIPAA, and PCI-DSS. Blockchain's immutability can create compliance challenges, as regulations often require organizations to modify or delete identity records in response to privacy concerns. To address this issue, decentralized identity frameworks must implement privacy-preserving techniques, such as zero-knowledge proofs (ZKPs) and selective disclosure mechanisms, which allow machine identities to prove their authenticity without revealing sensitive identity attributes.

The adoption of blockchain-based identity management also requires seamless integration with existing security infrastructure, including IAM platforms, PKI solutions, and cloud security frameworks. Organizations must ensure that blockchain-based machine identities can interoperate with traditional authentication mechanisms, enabling a gradual transition to decentralized identity models. Hybrid identity architectures, where blockchain coexists with traditional PKI and IAM systems, provide a pragmatic approach for enterprises looking to enhance machine identity security without completely replacing their existing security investments.

As blockchain technology matures, its role in decentralized machine identity management will continue to expand, offering enhanced security, transparency, and autonomy in identity verification. Organizations that adopt blockchain-based identity frameworks can reduce reliance on centralized authorities, mitigate identity fraud risks, and improve interoperability across distributed systems. While challenges remain in scalability, regulatory compliance, and integration, the potential benefits of decentralized machine identities make blockchain a transformative force in the future of identity security. As enterprises explore new ways to secure machine-to-machine interactions, blockchain will play a critical role in establishing trust, protecting sensitive credentials, and enabling secure digital ecosystems in an increasingly interconnected world.

Challenges in Scaling Machine Identity Management

As organizations expand their digital ecosystems, the number of machine identities they must manage grows at an exponential rate. The proliferation of cloud services, microservices architectures, DevOps workflows, and IoT devices has led to a surge in the number of machine identities, including API keys, digital certificates, service accounts, and cryptographic credentials. While machine identities enable secure authentication, encryption, and communication between systems, the challenge of managing them at scale has become a pressing concern for enterprises. The complexity of machine identity management increases with the need for automation, security, compliance, and lifecycle governance, creating multiple obstacles that organizations must address to maintain control over their expanding identity landscape.

One of the primary challenges in scaling machine identity management is visibility. Many organizations lack a centralized inventory of their machine identities, making it difficult to track where credentials are stored, who has access to them, and whether they comply with security policies. Machine identities are often distributed across different cloud platforms, on-premises infrastructure, and third-party applications, leading to identity sprawl. Without proper visibility, security teams struggle to detect orphaned identities, expired certificates, and misconfigured credentials that could be exploited by attackers. Gaining comprehensive visibility into all machine identities requires centralized identity discovery, continuous monitoring, and real-time reporting to prevent security gaps from emerging as organizations scale.

Automation plays a crucial role in scaling machine identity management, but implementing automation across diverse environments presents significant technical and operational challenges. Organizations must integrate automated identity provisioning, rotation, and revocation processes into their existing security frameworks without disrupting business operations. Many legacy systems still rely on manual identity management practices, making it difficult to transition to automated workflows without extensive system reconfiguration. In modern cloud environments, where thousands of machine identities are created and destroyed dynamically, automation must be capable of adapting to rapid changes in infrastructure while ensuring that security policies remain enforced. Without proper automation, machine identities can accumulate unmanaged, increasing the risk of unauthorized access and identity misuse.

The need for strong access controls and privilege management further complicates the scalability of machine identity security. As organizations scale their machine identities, enforcing the principle of least privilege becomes more challenging. Many machine identities are overprivileged, granting excessive access to systems, databases, and cloud services. Overprivileged machine identities increase the risk of credential compromise, as attackers can exploit them to gain unauthorized access to critical resources. Implementing role-based access control (RBAC) and attribute-based access control (ABAC) frameworks is essential for enforcing fine-grained access restrictions, but managing thousands or even millions of machine identities requires continuous policy enforcement and real-time access reviews. Organizations must integrate access control automation with machine identity governance to prevent privilege escalation and identity misuse.

Certificate lifecycle management is another major challenge in scaling machine identity security. Digital certificates are used to authenticate machines, secure communications, and encrypt sensitive data, but managing certificates across complex environments is increasingly difficult. Many organizations rely on multiple certificate authorities (CAs), leading to inconsistent certificate issuance, renewal, and revocation processes. Expired or misconfigured certificates can cause service outages, authentication failures, and security vulnerabilities, disrupting business operations. Automated certificate lifecycle management solutions help organizations scale certificate management by ensuring that all machine identities have valid, up-to-date credentials. However, implementing these solutions requires seamless integration with PKI infrastructures, DevOps pipelines, and cloud-native security frameworks to maintain consistency across all environments.

Compliance with regulatory standards adds another layer of complexity to scaling machine identity management. Organizations operating in highly regulated industries, such as finance, healthcare, and government, must adhere to strict security requirements for identity authentication, data encryption, and access logging. Regulations such as GDPR, HIPAA, PCI-DSS, and NIST mandate that organizations implement robust identity governance frameworks, maintain audit trails of identity-related activities, and enforce security policies to protect sensitive information. As organizations scale, ensuring that all machine identities comply with these regulations becomes increasingly difficult. Security teams must implement continuous compliance monitoring and automated policy enforcement to prevent violations and reduce the risk of regulatory penalties.

Another challenge in scaling machine identity management is the rapid expansion of cloud and multi-cloud environments. Organizations leveraging multiple cloud service providers must manage machine identities across different IAM frameworks, each with its own set of policies, authentication mechanisms, and security controls. Managing machine identities across AWS, Azure, Google Cloud, and private cloud environments requires a unified approach to identity governance, but achieving consistency across diverse cloud platforms remains a complex task. Many organizations struggle with identity fragmentation, where different teams use separate identity management tools, leading to a lack of standardization and increased security risks. Implementing cloud-native identity orchestration solutions helps organizations consolidate machine identity management across multi-cloud environments, but integration challenges and security misconfigurations must be carefully addressed.

Threat detection and incident response for machine identities become more difficult as organizations scale. Attackers frequently target machine identities as an entry point to infiltrate enterprise networks, impersonate trusted systems, and escalate privileges. Without real-time threat detection, organizations may fail to identify compromised credentials before they are exploited for malicious activities. Traditional security monitoring tools are often insufficient for detecting machine identity-related threats, as they primarily focus on human user authentication and behavior analytics. Implementing machine identity-specific threat intelligence, behavioral analytics, and automated incident response capabilities is essential for detecting and mitigating identity-based attacks at scale. Organizations must also enforce rapid credential revocation and key rotation mechanisms to minimize the impact of identity compromises.

Machine identity governance becomes increasingly complex as organizations adopt DevOps, CI/CD pipelines, and containerized environments. DevOps teams frequently generate machine identities for automated deployments, infrastructure provisioning, and microservices communication. However, without proper governance, these identities can proliferate uncontrollably, leading to security blind spots. Many DevOps teams prioritize speed and efficiency over security, resulting in hardcoded credentials, unmonitored API keys, and orphaned service accounts. Organizations must implement security controls that integrate seamlessly with DevOps workflows, ensuring that machine identities are created, managed, and decommissioned securely. Identity security automation must be embedded into CI/CD pipelines to enforce compliance and prevent identity-related vulnerabilities from being introduced during software development.

As machine identity security continues to scale, organizations must also address the growing challenge of quantum computing threats. Current cryptographic standards used in machine identity authentication and encryption will eventually become vulnerable to quantum attacks, necessitating a transition to quantum-resistant cryptographic algorithms. Organizations must prepare for this shift by adopting cryptographic agility, ensuring that their identity management frameworks can support post-quantum encryption techniques. The transition to quantum-safe machine identity management will require organizations to update PKI infrastructures, replace legacy cryptographic protocols, and integrate post-quantum identity authentication mechanisms into their security frameworks.

Scaling machine identity management requires a strategic approach that combines automation, access control enforcement, certificate lifecycle management, compliance monitoring, cloud identity governance, and threat intelligence integration. Organizations that fail to address these challenges risk identity sprawl, credential misuse, and security breaches that can disrupt critical business operations. By implementing proactive security measures, continuous monitoring, and automated policy enforcement, enterprises can effectively scale their machine identity management frameworks while maintaining strong security postures across their digital ecosystems.

Identity Federation and Cross-Enterprise Machine Trust

As digital ecosystems continue to expand, enterprises increasingly rely on interconnected networks, cloud services, and third-party providers to operate efficiently. This interconnectedness demands secure authentication and authorization mechanisms that allow machines from different organizations to trust each other without compromising security. Identity federation and cross-enterprise machine trust play a crucial role in enabling secure, seamless interactions between independent entities, ensuring that machine identities are verified, authenticated, and granted access based on established trust policies.

Identity federation allows organizations to establish trust relationships between different identity domains, enabling machine identities to be authenticated across multiple enterprises without requiring each entity to maintain separate credentials. Instead of managing distinct authentication processes for every external service or partner, organizations can leverage identity federation frameworks to enable single sign-on (SSO) for machines, APIs, and cloud workloads. This reduces identity fragmentation and simplifies access control, allowing machines from different enterprises to interact securely while maintaining compliance with security policies.

Cross-enterprise machine trust is essential for industries that rely on multi-party collaboration, such as supply chain management, financial services, healthcare, and telecommunications. In these sectors, organizations often need to share data, authenticate services, and authorize access to critical infrastructure across different organizations. Without a unified identity federation framework, each enterprise would have to manually manage access credentials, leading to inefficiencies, security risks, and administrative overhead. By implementing federated identity management, enterprises can establish shared trust mechanisms that enforce security policies while allowing seamless machine-to-machine communication.

Federated identity systems typically rely on standardized authentication protocols, such as Security Assertion Markup Language (SAML), OAuth 2.0, and OpenID Connect (OIDC). These protocols enable machines to authenticate across different domains by exchanging identity tokens, ensuring that access requests are validated without exposing sensitive credentials. For example, an enterprise running a cloud-based application that relies on multiple third-party APIs can use OAuth 2.0 to authenticate API requests across multiple service providers. Instead of each machine identity needing to store and manage separate credentials for every external service, OAuth allows them to present an access token issued by a trusted identity provider (IdP), ensuring a secure and scalable authentication process.

In multi-cloud environments, identity federation is crucial for maintaining consistent security policies across different cloud platforms. Enterprises operating in hybrid or multi-cloud infrastructures often use identity federation to enable cross-cloud authentication, ensuring that workloads running in AWS, Azure, and Google Cloud can securely communicate without relying on separate identity silos. Cloud providers offer identity federation capabilities through services such as AWS IAM Identity Center, Azure Active Directory B2B, and Google Cloud Identity Federation, allowing enterprises to extend their internal identity management policies to external cloud environments.

Establishing trust between machine identities across different enterprises requires the implementation of cryptographic trust mechanisms. Organizations must use digital certificates, cryptographic keys, and certificate authorities (CAs) to verify machine identities and prevent unauthorized access. Public key infrastructure (PKI) plays a central role in federated machine identity trust, allowing enterprises to issue, validate, and revoke digital certificates that authenticate machines across different security domains. By using a trusted CA, organizations can ensure that only authorized machine identities can participate in cross-enterprise communications.

One of the challenges of identity federation is managing trust relationships between independent organizations with different security policies, compliance requirements, and risk tolerances. Enterprises must establish clear governance frameworks that define how machine identities are issued, authenticated, and revoked within a federated environment. Trust agreements must outline security policies, encryption standards, and access control mechanisms to prevent unauthorized access or privilege escalation. Without well-defined governance models, identity federation can introduce security gaps that attackers may exploit to impersonate trusted machine identities.

Another key challenge in cross-enterprise machine trust is ensuring real-time identity verification and continuous monitoring. Machine identities that are federated across different organizations must be continuously validated to detect potential compromise or misuse. Organizations must implement identity monitoring tools that track authentication events, analyze behavioral patterns, and detect anomalies that could indicate unauthorized access attempts. Security information and event management (SIEM) solutions can aggregate identity-related logs across federated environments, providing real-time visibility into machine identity activity and enabling rapid response to potential security threats.

Zero trust security models enhance cross-enterprise machine trust by requiring continuous verification of machine identities, even within federated environments. Traditional identity federation frameworks assume that once an identity is authenticated by a trusted provider, it should be granted access without additional verification. However, zero trust principles dictate that machine identities should be continuously authenticated and authorized based on contextual risk assessments. This means that federated identities must be evaluated dynamically based on real-time factors such as device health, geographic location, behavioral patterns, and threat intelligence insights before access is granted.

Blockchain and decentralized identity frameworks are emerging as alternatives to traditional federated identity models. Instead of relying on centralized identity providers, blockchain-based identity solutions use distributed ledgers to verify machine identities in a decentralized manner. Decentralized identifiers (DIDs) enable machines to authenticate across different enterprises without relying on a single trusted authority. By leveraging blockchain, organizations can establish tamper-proof identity records that are cryptographically secured, reducing the risk of identity fraud and unauthorized access in cross-enterprise environments.

Regulatory compliance plays a critical role in federated machine identity management, particularly in industries such as finance, healthcare, and government. Regulations such as GDPR, HIPAA, PCI-DSS, and NIST require enterprises to implement strict identity governance policies that ensure machine identities are securely authenticated and managed. Compliance frameworks mandate that federated identity systems enforce encryption, access controls, and audit logging to prevent identity-related security breaches. Organizations participating in identity federation agreements must align their security policies with regulatory requirements to ensure that sensitive data remains protected across multiple enterprises.

Organizations must also address the issue of identity lifecycle management in federated environments. Machine identities that are shared across enterprises must follow consistent lifecycle policies, including issuance, renewal, and revocation. If a machine identity is no longer needed or becomes compromised, it must be revoked immediately to prevent unauthorized access. Automated certificate lifecycle management and just-in-time (JIT) credential provisioning can help enforce dynamic identity governance, ensuring that machine identities are granted access only when required and are deactivated when no longer needed.

The future of identity federation and cross-enterprise machine trust will be driven by advances in automation, artificial intelligence, and zero trust security models. AI-driven identity analytics will enhance identity verification by analyzing vast amounts of authentication data to detect suspicious activities and prevent identity fraud. Automated policy enforcement will enable enterprises to define and enforce trust relationships dynamically, ensuring that federated machine identities remain compliant with security standards. As enterprises continue to expand their digital operations, federated identity frameworks will play a critical role in securing machine-to-machine interactions, enabling secure collaboration across diverse industries, and protecting critical infrastructure from identity-based threats.

Implementing a Machine Identity Management Strategy

The rapid expansion of digital ecosystems, cloud computing, IoT devices, and automated processes has significantly increased the number of machine identities that organizations must manage. Machine identities, including digital certificates, API keys, cryptographic keys, service accounts, and tokens, play a critical role in securing machine-to-machine authentication, encryption, and access control. Without a well-defined machine identity management strategy, organizations risk identity sprawl, security breaches, compliance violations, and operational disruptions. Implementing a structured machine identity management strategy ensures that machine identities remain secure, properly governed, and efficiently integrated into enterprise security frameworks.

The first step in developing a machine identity management strategy is gaining visibility into all machine identities across the organization. Many enterprises struggle with identity sprawl, where machine identities are created, used, and forgotten without centralized oversight. A comprehensive inventory of all machine identities, their owners, their usage, and their expiration dates is essential for understanding the current identity landscape. Organizations should deploy automated discovery tools that scan infrastructure, cloud environments, repositories, and network configurations to identify all existing machine identities. This visibility allows security teams to assess risks, eliminate redundant identities, and prioritize security measures based on identity criticality.

Once visibility is established, organizations must implement standardized policies for machine identity issuance, renewal, and revocation. A structured policy framework ensures that machine identities follow security best practices, including strong authentication, encryption standards, and expiration timelines. Digital certificates, for example, should have predefined lifespans to prevent expired or misused certificates from lingering in enterprise environments. API keys should be issued with restricted scopes and usage limits to prevent unauthorized access. Service accounts must be granted only the necessary privileges based on the principle of least privilege, reducing the risk of credential misuse. Standardized policies create consistency across identity management processes, reducing administrative overhead while enhancing security posture.

Automation plays a crucial role in an effective machine identity management strategy. Manually managing thousands or even millions of machine identities is impractical and increases the risk of human error. Organizations should integrate automation tools that handle identity provisioning, renewal, rotation, and revocation without requiring manual intervention. Automated certificate lifecycle management ensures that digital certificates are renewed before expiration, preventing service disruptions. Just-in-time (JIT) identity provisioning enables temporary credential issuance that automatically expires after a predefined period, reducing the risk of long-lived credentials being compromised. Automated key rotation mechanisms enhance security by regularly refreshing cryptographic keys, ensuring that attackers cannot exploit stale credentials.

A centralized machine identity management platform provides a unified interface for managing and securing machine identities across the entire enterprise. Many organizations struggle with fragmented identity management due to the use of multiple security tools, cloud providers, and on-premises systems. A centralized platform consolidates identity governance, enforcing consistent policies across diverse environments. Identity and access management (IAM) solutions, certificate authorities (CAs), and secrets management tools should be integrated into a single system that allows security teams to monitor, manage, and audit machine identities efficiently. Centralization simplifies identity governance, enabling security teams to respond rapidly to identity-related incidents and policy violations.

Monitoring and auditing machine identities in real time are essential for detecting unauthorized access, anomalies, and potential breaches. Machine identities should be continuously tracked to identify suspicious authentication requests, excessive privilege escalations, and abnormal service-to-service communications. Security information and event management (SIEM) platforms aggregate machine identity logs, providing visibility into identity activity and potential threats. Behavioral analytics powered by artificial intelligence (AI) can detect deviations from normal identity behavior, flagging compromised credentials or unauthorized access attempts. Continuous monitoring strengthens an organization's security posture by ensuring that identity-related threats are identified and remediated before they lead to major security incidents.

Incident response and remediation processes must be included in a machine identity management strategy to address compromised or misused identities. Security teams should establish predefined workflows for handling machine identity breaches, ensuring that compromised credentials are revoked immediately, access logs are reviewed, and forensic investigations are conducted. Automated incident response platforms enable organizations to isolate affected machine identities, enforce containment measures, and mitigate security risks in real time. Integrating identity-related incidents into existing security operations centers (SOCs) improves an organization's ability to detect, respond to, and recover from identity-based threats.

Compliance with regulatory standards is a critical component of machine identity management. Organizations must ensure that machine identities adhere to industry regulations such as GDPR, HIPAA, PCI-DSS, NIST, and ISO 27001. Compliance mandates require organizations to enforce encryption policies, maintain access control logs, and implement strong authentication mechanisms for machine identities. Automated compliance reporting tools help organizations generate audit trails that demonstrate adherence to regulatory standards, reducing the risk of penalties and legal consequences. A well-defined compliance framework ensures that machine identity management aligns with both security best practices and regulatory requirements.

Integration with cloud-native security frameworks is necessary to secure machine identities in modern IT environments. As enterprises adopt multi-cloud and hybrid cloud infrastructures, managing machine identities across different cloud providers becomes increasingly complex. Cloud-native identity services such as AWS IAM,

Azure Managed Identities, and Google Cloud IAM provide built-in capabilities for managing machine identities within cloud environments. Organizations must ensure that their identity management strategy aligns with cloud security best practices, including workload identity federation, cloud-based certificate management, and role-based access control for cloud workloads. Seamless integration with cloud identity services enhances security while maintaining operational agility.

Educating teams and promoting awareness of machine identity security is essential for ensuring the success of an identity management strategy. Developers, DevOps teams, security professionals, and IT administrators must be trained on identity security best practices, including proper credential handling, secure API authentication, and certificate management. Security awareness programs should emphasize the risks of hardcoded credentials, overprivileged service accounts, and identity misconfigurations. Enforcing security policies through training and awareness ensures that all teams within an organization contribute to a robust machine identity security framework.

Machine identity governance must continuously evolve to keep pace with emerging threats and technological advancements. Organizations should conduct periodic reviews of their identity management strategy, assessing the effectiveness of existing security controls, automation processes, and compliance measures. Regular security audits help identify gaps in identity governance, enabling organizations to refine policies, improve automation, and enhance security monitoring. Threat intelligence integration allows organizations to stay ahead of emerging machine identity attack vectors, ensuring that their security frameworks remain resilient against evolving cyber threats.

Implementing a machine identity management strategy requires a combination of visibility, automation, policy enforcement, monitoring, incident response, compliance alignment, and continuous improvement. As machine identities become an increasingly critical component of enterprise security, organizations must prioritize identity governance to prevent unauthorized access, mitigate security risks, and maintain trust in their digital ecosystems. By adopting a proactive approach to machine identity security, enterprises can safeguard their infrastructure, protect sensitive data, and ensure that machine-to-machine interactions remain secure, reliable, and resilient in an ever-changing cybersecurity landscape.

The Role of Identity and Access Management (IAM) in Machine Identity

Identity and Access Management (IAM) is a fundamental pillar of cybersecurity, ensuring that only authorized entities—whether human users or machines—can access enterprise resources. While IAM has traditionally been associated with managing human identities, the growing reliance on automation, cloud computing, and machine-to-machine communication has expanded its role to include machine identities. Machine identities, which include API keys, digital certificates, service accounts, and cryptographic tokens, require the same level of governance and security controls as human identities. IAM frameworks provide the necessary tools, policies, and enforcement mechanisms to manage, authenticate, and authorize machine identities, ensuring that they operate securely within enterprise environments.

Machine identities play a critical role in securing digital transactions, encrypting data transmissions, and verifying service-to-service communications. However, as organizations deploy more cloud-based workloads, IoT devices, and containerized applications, the number of machine identities in use has grown exponentially. This rapid expansion makes it difficult for enterprises to track, manage, and protect all machine identities effectively. Without proper IAM controls, machine identities can be mismanaged, overprivileged, or left unmonitored, increasing the risk of unauthorized access, credential misuse, and identity-based cyberattacks. Implementing IAM policies specifically tailored for machine identities is essential to mitigate these risks and enforce security best practices across the organization.

IAM solutions provide centralized identity governance that enables organizations to establish standardized policies for issuing, rotating, and revoking machine identities. Unlike human identities, which rely on username-password authentication, machine identities use cryptographic credentials such as API tokens and digital certificates to establish trust. IAM frameworks integrate with public key infrastructure (PKI), certificate authorities (CAs), and secrets management platforms to automate the lifecycle management of these identities. Automated IAM policies ensure that machine identities adhere to security best practices, such as periodic key rotation, certificate renewal, and just-in-time (JIT) credential provisioning, reducing the likelihood of credential compromise.

Access control is a core function of IAM in machine identity security, enforcing fine-grained permissions based on the principle of least privilege. Many organizations struggle with overprivileged machine identities that have access to more resources than necessary. Excessive privileges increase the attack surface, allowing attackers to exploit compromised machine identities to move laterally within enterprise networks. IAM frameworks use role-based access control (RBAC) and attribute-based access control (ABAC) to restrict machine identity permissions, ensuring that each identity has only the access required for its specific function. Implementing IAM-driven access policies prevents privilege escalation, unauthorized data access, and service disruptions caused by misconfigured machine identities.

IAM plays a vital role in securing cloud environments, where machine identities are used extensively to authenticate workloads, microservices, and virtual machines. Cloud providers offer native IAM services, such as AWS IAM, Azure Active Directory, and Google Cloud IAM, which help organizations manage machine identities across multi-cloud environments. These IAM solutions enable enterprises to define identity federation policies, enforce multi-factor authentication (MFA) for machine identities, and implement identity-aware networking. By leveraging cloud-native IAM capabilities, organizations can maintain consistent security policies across different cloud platforms while ensuring that machine identities are authenticated and authorized dynamically.

Zero trust security models enhance the role of IAM in machine identity management by requiring continuous authentication and authorization for all machine-to-machine interactions. Traditional security models assume implicit trust for machine identities that have already been authenticated, but zero trust eliminates this assumption by enforcing verification at every access request. IAM solutions integrated with zero trust architectures assess contextual factors such as identity behavior, network location, and security posture before granting access to resources. Continuous identity verification helps detect anomalies, mitigate insider threats, and prevent unauthorized access by compromised machine identities.

IAM solutions also support machine identity monitoring and anomaly detection by integrating with security information and event management (SIEM) platforms. Continuous monitoring of machine identity activity allows organizations to detect suspicious authentication attempts, excessive API calls, and unauthorized privilege escalations. Machine learning-driven behavioral analytics can identify deviations from normal identity usage, flagging potential identity compromises in real time. IAM-driven identity analytics provide organizations with actionable insights, enabling security teams to revoke compromised credentials, block unauthorized access attempts, and enforce incident response measures before attackers exploit machine identities for malicious purposes.

Federated identity management enables IAM frameworks to establish cross-enterprise trust for machine identities, allowing organizations to authenticate machines across multiple security domains. Many enterprises rely on third-party service providers, cloud vendors, and business partners to operate critical applications and services. Federated IAM policies allow machine identities to authenticate seamlessly across these entities without requiring separate credentials for each system. Secure token exchange protocols such as OAuth 2.0, SAML, and OpenID Connect facilitate federated machine identity authentication, ensuring that machines can interact securely across different organizations while maintaining strong access controls.

IAM also plays a key role in securing DevOps environments, where machine identities are frequently used to automate infrastructure deployments, CI/CD pipelines, and software integrations. In DevOps workflows, IAM solutions integrate with secrets management tools such as HashiCorp Vault, AWS Secrets Manager, and Azure Key Vault to secure API keys, cryptographic tokens, and SSH credentials used by automation scripts. IAM-driven secrets management ensures that machine identities do not rely on hardcoded credentials, which can be accidentally exposed in source code repositories. Enforcing IAM security policies within DevOps pipelines prevents credential leaks, enforces temporary access restrictions, and enhances the security of automated processes.

Compliance with regulatory requirements is another critical function of IAM in machine identity management. Industry regulations such as GDPR, HIPAA, PCI-DSS, and NIST mandate that organizations implement strong authentication, encryption, and access control mechanisms for all identities, including machine identities. IAM frameworks provide audit logging and reporting capabilities that help organizations maintain compliance by tracking machine identity activity, access requests, and security incidents. Automated IAM compliance enforcement ensures that machine identity policies align with regulatory standards, reducing the risk of non-compliance penalties and security breaches.

Incident response and remediation workflows benefit from IAM-driven machine identity management by enabling rapid response to identity-related security threats. When a machine identity is suspected of being compromised, IAM solutions allow security teams to revoke credentials, disable access, and isolate affected workloads immediately. Automated IAM policies can enforce credential rotation, requiring machines to reauthenticate using newly issued identities before regaining access. Integrating IAM with security orchestration, automation, and response (SOAR) platforms enables organizations to contain machine identity breaches efficiently, minimizing the impact of cyberattacks on critical systems.

As organizations continue to expand their digital operations, IAM will remain a foundational component of machine identity security. By implementing centralized identity governance, enforcing least privilege access controls, integrating continuous monitoring, and leveraging zero trust security models, enterprises can strengthen machine identity protection and reduce the risks associated with unauthorized access. IAM solutions provide the scalability, automation, and security intelligence necessary to manage machine identities effectively, ensuring that they remain secure, compliant, and resilient in an increasingly interconnected digital ecosystem.

Secrets Rotations and Certificate Renewals

As organizations expand their digital operations, the number of secrets and cryptographic certificates they must manage increases exponentially. Secrets, including API keys, database credentials, encryption keys, and service tokens, enable secure authentication and communication between machines, applications, and cloud services. Digital certificates provide cryptographic assurance that machine identities are trusted and authorized to access enterprise resources. However, without proper lifecycle management, secrets and certificates can become a significant security liability. Failure to rotate secrets regularly or renew certificates before expiration can lead to unauthorized access, service disruptions, and security breaches. Implementing a structured strategy for secrets rotation and certificate renewal is essential for maintaining security, compliance, and operational resilience.

Secrets rotation refers to the automated or scheduled process of periodically replacing authentication credentials to minimize the risk of credential exposure. Many organizations fail to rotate secrets regularly, leaving sensitive credentials in use for extended periods. Static or long-lived secrets create an attractive target for attackers, who can exploit compromised credentials to gain persistent access to enterprise systems. By implementing automatic secrets rotation policies, organizations can reduce the risk of credential misuse while ensuring that machine identities always authenticate using secure, up-to-date credentials.

Secrets rotation is particularly important in DevOps environments, where automated pipelines, microservices, and infrastructure-as-code (IaC) deployments frequently interact using secrets. Hardcoded credentials in configuration files, scripts, or version control systems pose a serious security risk. If an attacker gains access to a repository containing plaintext secrets, they can exploit them to escalate privileges, move laterally across networks, or extract sensitive data.

Secrets management solutions, such as HashiCorp Vault, AWS Secrets Manager, and Azure Key Vault, provide centralized secret storage, encryption, and automatic rotation capabilities, ensuring that secrets are never exposed or stored insecurely.

The frequency of secrets rotation depends on the sensitivity and risk level associated with each credential. High-risk secrets, such as API keys with administrative privileges or database credentials used for financial transactions, should be rotated more frequently than lower-risk secrets. Organizations should enforce secrets rotation policies based on security best practices, regulatory requirements, and industry standards. Just-in-time (JIT) access provisioning further enhances security by generating temporary secrets that expire automatically after a defined period, ensuring that long-lived credentials are eliminated from the system.

Certificate renewals play a similarly critical role in maintaining security across enterprise networks. Digital certificates authenticate machine identities, encrypt communications, and prevent man-in-the-middle (MITM) attacks. However, certificates have a predefined expiration period, after which they must be renewed to remain valid. Expired certificates can cause service outages, authentication failures, and security vulnerabilities. Many organizations struggle with certificate management due to the sheer volume of certificates in use, leading to a lack of visibility into expiration dates and renewal processes.

Automated certificate lifecycle management is essential for preventing expired certificates from disrupting operations. Certificate automation platforms integrate with certificate authorities (CAs) to issue, renew, and revoke certificates without manual intervention. Organizations can use tools such as Let's Encrypt, Venafi, DigiCert, and AWS Certificate Manager to automate certificate renewals, ensuring that all machine identities maintain valid cryptographic credentials. By implementing automated renewal workflows, enterprises can eliminate the risk of expired certificates causing unexpected downtime.

Certificate expiration monitoring is another key component of certificate renewal strategies. Security teams must track certificate lifespans and receive alerts before expiration to prevent disruptions. A centralized certificate inventory provides visibility into all active certificates, their expiration dates, and their issuing authorities. Automated certificate expiration alerts notify administrators in advance, allowing them to renew or replace certificates before they expire. Continuous monitoring of certificate usage helps detect anomalies, such as unauthorized certificate issuance or certificate misuse by malicious actors.

Organizations must also ensure that certificate revocation mechanisms are in place to respond to compromised or misused certificates. If a private key associated with a certificate is leaked, an attacker can use the certificate to impersonate trusted systems. Certificate revocation lists (CRLs) and Online Certificate Status Protocol (OCSP) mechanisms enable organizations to revoke compromised certificates and prevent unauthorized entities from using them. Automated revocation workflows help security teams respond quickly to certificate compromises, reducing the risk of identity spoofing and fraudulent activities.

In cloud-native environments, certificate renewals and secrets rotations become even more complex due to the dynamic nature of containerized workloads, serverless functions, and ephemeral computing resources. Traditional certificate management processes may not be sufficient for securing cloud-native applications, where machine identities frequently change. Kubernetes-native certificate management solutions, such as cert-manager and Istio, enable automated certificate provisioning, renewal, and rotation for containerized applications. These tools integrate with cloud-native service meshes and ingress controllers, ensuring that encrypted communication remains secure even as workloads scale dynamically.

Regulatory compliance frameworks mandate strict controls for secrets management and certificate lifecycle processes. Regulations such as GDPR, HIPAA, PCI-DSS, and NIST require organizations to enforce encryption, authentication, and access control measures for machine identities. Compliance audits often include verification of secrets rotation policies, certificate expiration tracking, and revocation procedures. Automated compliance reporting tools provide audit logs that demonstrate adherence to security policies, helping organizations maintain regulatory compliance while minimizing the risk of security violations.

The adoption of zero trust security models further reinforces the importance of secrets rotation and certificate renewals. Zero trust principles require continuous verification of all identities, whether human or machine, before granting access to enterprise resources. Rotating secrets and renewing certificates align with zero trust by ensuring that authentication credentials remain valid, up to date, and resistant to compromise. Dynamic identity validation, coupled with automated identity governance, strengthens security by preventing attackers from exploiting stale or exposed credentials.

Organizations must also implement access control policies that restrict how secrets and certificates are used. Role-based access control (RBAC) and attribute-based access control (ABAC) frameworks define which users, applications, and services can access specific credentials. Least privilege enforcement ensures that secrets are accessible only to authorized entities that require them for legitimate operations. Machine identity analytics provide insights into credential usage patterns, enabling security teams to detect suspicious activity, revoke compromised credentials, and enforce stricter access policies.

Continuous improvement in secrets rotation and certificate renewal strategies is necessary to keep pace with evolving security threats. Organizations must periodically review and refine their identity management policies, ensuring that secrets rotation frequencies align with emerging cybersecurity risks. Security teams should conduct penetration testing and red teaming exercises to identify potential weaknesses in credential management processes. By simulating attack scenarios, organizations can assess their ability to respond to compromised credentials, test automated response mechanisms, and strengthen their security posture.

As digital transformation accelerates, the ability to manage secrets rotations and certificate renewals efficiently will become a critical aspect of enterprise security. Organizations that implement automated identity lifecycle management, proactive monitoring, and compliance-driven security policies will be better equipped to mitigate credential-based threats, prevent service disruptions, and maintain trust in their machine identities. By prioritizing secrets rotation and certificate renewal as core security practices, enterprises can ensure that their authentication mechanisms remain robust, resilient, and resistant to evolving cyber threats.

Implementing Least Privilege for Machine Identities

As organizations continue to automate processes, integrate cloud services, and deploy complex digital infrastructures, the number of machine identities within enterprise environments has grown exponentially. Machine identities, including service accounts, API keys, cryptographic certificates, SSH keys, and workload identities, authenticate and authorize machines, applications, and services to interact securely. However, if machine identities are not properly managed, they can become overprivileged, granting excessive access to critical resources and increasing the risk of cyber threats. Implementing the principle of least privilege (PoLP) for machine identities is essential to minimizing security risks, reducing the attack surface, and preventing unauthorized access to sensitive systems.

Least privilege is a security principle that dictates that an identity—whether human or machine—should be granted only the minimum permissions necessary to perform its required functions. Overprivileged machine identities create significant security vulnerabilities, as attackers who compromise them can escalate privileges, move laterally within the network, and gain access to sensitive data. By enforcing least privilege access controls, organizations ensure that machine identities operate with restricted permissions, limiting the potential damage in the event of a security breach.

The first step in implementing least privilege for machine identities is conducting a comprehensive inventory of all identities within the organization. Many enterprises lack visibility into the total number of machine identities in use, making it difficult to assess privilege levels and enforce appropriate restrictions. Automated discovery tools can help identify service accounts, API keys, SSH credentials, and workload identities across cloud environments, on-premises systems, and containerized applications. By mapping machine identities to their associated permissions, security teams can evaluate whether certain identities have excessive or unnecessary access.

Once visibility is established, organizations must analyze machine identity permissions to determine whether they align with operational needs. Many machine identities are created with default or overly broad permissions, granting them access to more resources than necessary. For example, a cloud service account may have administrator privileges when it only needs read access to specific storage buckets. Similarly, an API key used for inter-service communication may have unrestricted access to multiple endpoints when it only requires access to a single function. Security teams must assess these permission levels and apply least privilege principles by removing unnecessary access rights.

Role-based access control (RBAC) is a key mechanism for enforcing least privilege for machine identities. RBAC assigns permissions based on predefined roles, ensuring that machine identities are only granted access to the resources required for their designated functions. For example, a service account running an application in a cloud environment can be assigned a role that allows it to access a specific database but prevents it from modifying security settings. Organizations must define clear roles and policies that categorize machine identities based on their intended usage, restricting them from performing unauthorized actions.

Attribute-based access control (ABAC) provides a more dynamic approach to enforcing least privilege by evaluating contextual attributes before granting access. ABAC policies consider factors such as identity type, location, authentication method, and behavioral patterns when determining access permissions. For example, a machine identity that typically accesses a cloud service from a specific IP range may be denied access if it attempts authentication from an unexpected location. Implementing ABAC allows organizations to apply granular access restrictions based on real-time conditions, enhancing security while maintaining operational flexibility.

Just-in-time (JIT) access controls further strengthen least privilege by granting machine identities temporary privileges only when needed. Instead of maintaining persistent access to critical systems, machine identities receive permissions for a limited time and are automatically revoked once their function is complete. JIT access policies reduce the window of opportunity for attackers who may attempt to exploit compromised credentials. Cloud platforms and identity management solutions support JIT access by allowing administrators to configure time-bound access permissions for machine identities performing specific tasks.

Machine identity lifecycle management plays a crucial role in enforcing least privilege. Many organizations struggle with identity sprawl, where machine identities accumulate over time without proper oversight. Orphaned identities—those that are no longer in use but still retain privileges—pose a significant security risk, as they can be exploited for unauthorized access. Organizations must establish automated identity governance processes that regularly review, rotate, and revoke machine identities based on usage patterns. Implementing periodic access reviews ensures that machine identities do not retain unnecessary permissions beyond their required lifespan.

Audit logging and monitoring are essential for detecting privilege misconfigurations and identifying unauthorized access attempts. Security teams must continuously track machine identity authentication events, API calls, and privilege escalations to detect anomalies that may indicate a security breach. SIEM (Security Information and Event Management) platforms collect identity-related logs and generate alerts for suspicious activity, allowing security teams to investigate and respond to potential threats. Behavioral analytics powered by artificial intelligence can further enhance security by identifying deviations from normal identity usage, enabling proactive privilege enforcement.

Enforcing least privilege for machine identities requires seamless integration with cloud identity and access management (IAM) solutions. Cloud providers such as AWS, Azure, and Google Cloud offer built-in IAM services that allow organizations to define fine-grained permissions for machine identities. Organizations must ensure that IAM policies are properly configured to restrict access based on business requirements. Misconfigured IAM roles with excessive privileges are a common cause of cloud security breaches, making it essential to audit and refine access policies regularly.

Zero trust security models enhance least privilege by requiring continuous authentication and authorization for all machine identities. Traditional security models assume that once an identity is authenticated, it should be trusted indefinitely. Zero trust eliminates this assumption by enforcing identity verification at every access request, regardless of whether the identity originates from inside or outside the network. Implementing zero trust for machine identities ensures that access permissions are granted dynamically based on real-time security assessments, reducing the risk of identity misuse.

Privileged access management (PAM) solutions help enforce least privilege for high-risk machine identities with administrative privileges. PAM solutions provide controlled access to sensitive resources, requiring additional verification before granting elevated permissions. Machine identities with privileged access should be subject to strict logging, session monitoring, and multi-factor authentication (MFA) to prevent unauthorized privilege escalation. By integrating PAM with machine identity management, organizations can secure critical assets while maintaining strict access control.

Regulatory compliance frameworks, including GDPR, HIPAA, PCI-DSS, and NIST, emphasize the importance of enforcing least privilege for all identities, including machine identities. Organizations must ensure that their access control policies align with regulatory requirements to avoid compliance violations. Automated compliance auditing tools help organizations track privilege assignments, generate access control reports, and enforce corrective actions when overprivileged identities are detected.

Continuous improvement is necessary to maintain an effective least privilege strategy for machine identities. Organizations should conduct regular privilege audits, review identity access policies, and refine access control mechanisms based on emerging threats and security best practices. Security teams must collaborate with DevOps, cloud architects, and compliance teams to ensure that least privilege enforcement remains a priority across all digital environments.

By implementing least privilege for machine identities, organizations can significantly reduce the attack surface, mitigate identity-related risks, and maintain strong access control across their IT ecosystems. Enforcing strict privilege policies, leveraging automated identity governance, and integrating real-time security monitoring ensure that machine identities operate securely while minimizing exposure to unauthorized access and privilege escalation attacks.

Preventing Machine Identity Exploitation by Cybercriminals

As organizations rely more heavily on automation, cloud computing, and interconnected systems, machine identities have become a prime target for cybercriminals. Unlike human identities, which are often protected by multi-factor authentication and strict access policies, machine identities are frequently overlooked or mismanaged. These identities, which include API keys, cryptographic certificates, SSH keys, and service accounts, enable secure communication between applications, servers, and cloud environments. However, when improperly managed or exposed, they provide attackers with an entry point for data theft, lateral movement, and persistent access within enterprise networks. Preventing machine identity exploitation requires a proactive approach to securing, monitoring, and managing these critical digital credentials.

One of the primary ways cybercriminals exploit machine identities is through stolen or leaked credentials. API keys and authentication tokens are often hardcoded into applications, configuration files, or repositories, making them easy targets for attackers. If these credentials are exposed in public code repositories, such as GitHub, attackers can quickly obtain them and use them to impersonate legitimate services, access sensitive data, or manipulate business logic. Organizations must enforce strict secrets management policies, ensuring that machine credentials are never stored in plaintext or embedded in code. Using dedicated secrets management solutions, such as HashiCorp Vault, AWS Secrets Manager, or Azure Key Vault, helps protect machine identities by securely storing and rotating credentials.

Another significant risk arises from overprivileged machine identities that have excessive access to enterprise resources. Many organizations assign broad permissions to machine identities to simplify system integration, but this creates security vulnerabilities. If a cybercriminal compromises an overprivileged machine identity, they can exploit its permissions to move laterally across the network, access critical databases, and execute malicious operations. Implementing least privilege access controls is essential to reducing this risk. Machine identities should only have the minimum necessary permissions to perform their designated functions, and security teams must regularly review access policies to eliminate unnecessary privileges.

Cybercriminals also exploit machine identities through expired or misconfigured digital certificates. Certificates authenticate machine identities and encrypt data transmissions, ensuring secure communications between servers, APIs, and cloud workloads. However, if certificates are not properly managed, they can create security gaps. Expired certificates cause authentication failures, leading administrators to bypass security controls temporarily, creating opportunities for attackers to exploit weak authentication mechanisms. Additionally, misconfigured certificates can be intercepted or spoofed, allowing attackers to perform man-in-the-middle (MITM) attacks. Automated certificate lifecycle management solutions help organizations prevent such risks by ensuring that certificates are issued, renewed, and revoked according to security best practices.

Machine identity exploitation is also facilitated by inadequate monitoring and logging of authentication events. Attackers often attempt to brute-force API keys, test stolen credentials, or exploit misconfigured access controls to gain unauthorized access. Without proper logging and real-time monitoring, these activities can go undetected until significant damage has been done. Implementing security information and event management (SIEM) solutions allows organizations to monitor authentication attempts, detect anomalies, and flag unauthorized access attempts. AI-driven behavioral analytics further enhance detection capabilities by identifying deviations from normal machine identity behavior, such as unusual access locations, excessive authentication failures, or unexpected privilege escalations.

Compromised machine identities are frequently used in supply chain attacks, where attackers exploit trusted third-party integrations to infiltrate enterprise networks. Many organizations rely on third-party services, SaaS applications, and cloud providers that use machine identities for authentication. If a third-party provider's machine identity is compromised, attackers can use it to gain access to customer environments, distribute malware, or intercept sensitive data. To mitigate this risk, organizations must enforce strict identity verification for third-party integrations, requiring mutual TLS (mTLS) authentication, signed API requests, and continuous trust evaluation. Supply chain security assessments should also include machine identity audits to ensure that third-party services adhere to strong identity management practices.

Cybercriminals also exploit machine identities through misconfigured cloud permissions and identity federation errors. Cloud platforms provide built-in identity and access management (IAM) features that control how machine identities interact with cloud resources. However, misconfigured IAM roles, excessive permissions, and weak authentication settings expose cloud-based machine identities to cyber threats. Attackers often target publicly exposed cloud APIs, weakly secured service accounts, and improperly configured identity federation settings to gain unauthorized access. Organizations must enforce strict IAM policies, apply conditional access rules, and implement just-in-time (JIT) credential provisioning to reduce the attack surface of cloud-based machine identities.

Insider threats further increase the risk of machine identity exploitation. Malicious insiders, disgruntled employees, or compromised internal accounts can misuse machine identities to access unauthorized data, disable security controls, or exfiltrate sensitive information. Enforcing machine identity governance policies helps mitigate insider threats by tracking identity usage, implementing access request approvals, and preventing unauthorized identity modifications. Role-based access control (RBAC) and attribute-based access control (ABAC) frameworks allow organizations to define granular permissions, ensuring that machine identities cannot be misused by insiders for malicious purposes.

Another emerging threat involves quantum computing, which has the potential to break cryptographic algorithms used in machine identity authentication. While large-scale quantum computers are not yet widely available, cybercriminals and nation-state actors are already collecting encrypted data in anticipation of future quantum decryption capabilities. Organizations must begin transitioning to quantum-resistant cryptographic algorithms to future-proof machine identity security. Post-quantum cryptographic standards, such as those being developed by NIST, will play a crucial role in protecting machine identities from quantum-enabled attacks.

Preventing machine identity exploitation requires continuous security assessments, regular audits, and policy enforcement. Organizations should implement automated identity lifecycle management to track the creation, usage, and expiration of machine identities. Identity governance frameworks help ensure that machine identities are properly assigned, monitored, and revoked when no longer needed. Automated policy enforcement tools allow security teams to define and enforce identity security policies across hybrid and multi-cloud environments, ensuring consistent protection for machine identities regardless of where they are deployed.

Incident response planning is essential for mitigating machine identity compromises. Organizations must establish predefined workflows for detecting, containing, and remediating identity-related security incidents. When a machine identity is suspected of being compromised, security teams should immediately revoke the credential, rotate associated keys, and investigate related access logs to determine the extent of the breach. Automated incident response platforms can accelerate containment efforts by enforcing access restrictions, triggering forensic analysis, and initiating credential revocation without manual intervention.

The increasing sophistication of cyber threats targeting machine identities requires organizations to adopt a proactive security strategy. By implementing strong access controls, continuous monitoring, automated identity governance, and advanced threat detection, enterprises can significantly reduce the risk of machine identity exploitation. Security teams must remain vigilant, continuously improving identity management practices to stay ahead of evolving cyber threats. Organizations that prioritize machine identity security will be better equipped to defend against credential-based attacks, ensuring the integrity, confidentiality, and availability of their digital infrastructure.

Case Studies: Machine Identity Breaches and Lessons Learned

Machine identity breaches have emerged as a significant threat to enterprise security, often enabling attackers to bypass traditional authentication mechanisms, move laterally within networks, and gain persistent access to critical systems. Unlike human identities, which benefit from multi-factor authentication and behavioral monitoring, machine identities are often unmanaged, overprivileged, or left unmonitored, making them attractive targets for cybercriminals. By analyzing past machine identity breaches, organizations can extract valuable lessons to strengthen their security posture and mitigate future threats. Several high-profile incidents illustrate the dangers associated with poor machine identity management and highlight best practices that enterprises must adopt.

One of the most widely discussed machine identity breaches occurred during the infamous SolarWinds supply chain attack. In this incident, attackers infiltrated the software development environment of SolarWinds, a major IT management company, and injected a backdoor into their Orion software updates. The attackers leveraged stolen or misused machine identities, including digital certificates and authentication tokens, to distribute malicious updates to thousands of customers, including government agencies and Fortune 500 companies. Because the malicious software was signed with a legitimate digital certificate, it evaded security detection mechanisms and was trusted by endpoint security solutions.

The key lesson from the SolarWinds breach is the importance of securing software supply chains and machine identities used in development environments. Organizations must implement strict code-signing policies, ensuring that digital certificates are properly managed and not used to sign unauthorized software. Automated certificate lifecycle management can prevent compromised or expired certificates from being misused in attacks. Additionally, zero trust security models should be enforced to verify every machine identity accessing development pipelines, reducing the risk of unauthorized access. Supply chain security assessments and continuous integrity monitoring of software updates can help detect anomalies before they impact customers.

Another major breach involving machine identities occurred when attackers exploited misconfigured AWS IAM roles to access sensitive cloud workloads. In this case, a misconfigured machine identity, originally intended for internal use, was left exposed with excessive permissions. The attackers discovered this overprivileged IAM role and used it to escalate access across multiple cloud services, ultimately exfiltrating sensitive customer data. The breach went undetected for weeks because the compromised machine identity was operating under legitimate credentials, making it difficult to differentiate from normal activity.

This incident underscores the critical need for enforcing least privilege access for machine identities. Organizations must conduct periodic privilege audits to identify and eliminate overprivileged IAM roles, API keys, and service accounts. Implementing just-in-time (JIT) access policies ensures that machine identities only receive temporary privileges when needed, reducing the attack surface. Additionally, real-time monitoring of cloud IAM activities, including anomaly detection for privilege escalations and excessive API calls, can help detect suspicious identity usage before an attack escalates. Cloud security posture management (CSPM) tools can further enhance visibility into identity misconfigurations and enforce policy-driven remediation.

Another example of machine identity exploitation involved an API key leak that led to a major data breach at a fintech company. The organization relied heavily on APIs to facilitate secure transactions, but a critical API key was accidentally embedded in a public GitHub repository. Attackers discovered the exposed key and used it to authenticate as a trusted service, executing fraudulent transactions and extracting financial data from customer accounts. The breach resulted in millions of dollars in fraudulent activity before security teams detected and revoked the compromised key.

This breach highlights the dangers of hardcoded secrets and emphasizes the need for automated secrets management. Organizations should enforce strict policies prohibiting developers from embedding secrets in code and must integrate secrets management solutions that automatically store, rotate, and revoke API keys. Implementing continuous scanning tools that detect and alert on exposed secrets in repositories, logs, and configuration files can prevent accidental credential leaks. Developers should also be trained on secure coding practices to ensure that machine identities are properly handled in software development environments.

A widely known incident involving digital certificate misuse occurred when attackers compromised a certificate authority (CA) and issued fraudulent certificates for major websites. By gaining control over the CA's signing infrastructure, the attackers generated trusted but illegitimate certificates, which allowed them to impersonate banking and email services. This enabled them to conduct man-in-the-middle (MITM) attacks, intercepting encrypted communications and stealing login credentials. The breach led to widespread security concerns, forcing organizations to revoke and replace thousands of compromised certificates.

This case highlights the importance of strong certificate authority security and continuous certificate monitoring. Organizations must implement certificate transparency logs to track and verify the issuance of digital certificates, ensuring that unauthorized certificates are detected immediately. Automated certificate revocation mechanisms must be in place to prevent malicious certificates from being used once identified. Additionally, mutual TLS (mTLS) should be adopted for service-to-service authentication, ensuring that both parties verify each other's identity using trusted certificates. Strengthening CA security through hardware security modules (HSMs) and strict key management practices can also prevent unauthorized certificate issuance.

One of the largest cyber-espionage campaigns in recent years involved machine identity exploitation in an advanced persistent threat (APT) attack. State-sponsored attackers infiltrated a global technology company by compromising an SSH key that was reused across multiple critical systems. Once inside, the attackers used the stolen key to access privileged systems, exfiltrate intellectual property, and maintain persistent access for months without detection. Because SSH keys are often treated as static credentials, security teams failed to rotate or monitor them effectively, allowing the attackers to operate undetected.

This attack demonstrates the need for automated SSH key rotation and strict access controls. Organizations must implement key management policies that enforce regular SSH key rotation and prohibit key reuse across different environments. Role-based access control (RBAC) and attribute-based access control (ABAC) should be applied to limit SSH key usage to only authorized systems. Continuous SSH session monitoring and logging can help detect unauthorized access attempts, while automated anomaly detection can identify unusual SSH activity that may indicate a compromised key.

Lessons from these breaches emphasize the importance of machine identity governance, proactive monitoring, and automation in identity lifecycle management. Organizations must treat machine identities with the same level of security as human identities, implementing strong authentication, least privilege access, continuous monitoring, and automated remediation for compromised credentials. Security teams should integrate identity security into incident response playbooks, ensuring that compromised machine identities can be revoked, rotated, and investigated efficiently.

By studying past machine identity breaches, organizations can strengthen their security strategies and reduce the risk of falling victim to similar attacks. Implementing identity-first security principles, adopting zero trust models, and leveraging automated identity management solutions will help enterprises stay ahead of evolving threats, ensuring that machine identities remain secure in an increasingly digital and interconnected world.

Best Practices for Large-Scale Enterprises

Managing machine identities at scale presents significant challenges for large enterprises that operate in complex, multi-cloud, and hybrid environments. As organizations expand their digital footprint, the number of machine identities—including API keys, digital certificates, service accounts, and cryptographic tokens—grows exponentially. Without a structured identity management strategy, enterprises risk credential sprawl, security breaches, and operational inefficiencies. Implementing best practices for machine identity management ensures that organizations maintain strong security postures, comply with regulatory standards, and enable secure, automated processes across their IT ecosystems.

The foundation of effective machine identity management in large-scale enterprises begins with comprehensive visibility. Many organizations struggle with identifying and cataloging all machine identities in use, leading to unmanaged credentials that pose security risks. Enterprises must deploy automated discovery tools that continuously scan infrastructure, cloud environments, and application ecosystems to identify active machine identities. Maintaining a centralized inventory of all machine identities, including their purpose, expiration dates, and ownership, helps security teams track and manage identities effectively.

Once visibility is established, organizations must implement strict governance policies to control the lifecycle of machine identities. Machine identities should be provisioned based on predefined security policies that dictate access levels, expiration timelines, and renewal processes. Automated lifecycle management ensures that certificates, API keys, and secrets are issued, rotated, and revoked dynamically, reducing the risk of outdated or misconfigured credentials being exploited by attackers. Enterprises should enforce policy-driven identity management, integrating identity governance platforms that apply consistent security rules across all environments.

Large-scale enterprises must adopt the principle of least privilege to minimize the risk of overprivileged machine identities. Excessive permissions create an expanded attack surface, allowing attackers to exploit compromised credentials to move laterally within networks.

Role-based access control (RBAC) and attribute-based access control (ABAC) should be implemented to restrict machine identity permissions based on operational requirements. Service accounts and API keys should be granted only the minimum access necessary to perform their intended functions. Periodic privilege audits help identify overprivileged identities and enforce corrective actions to reduce exposure.

Automation is essential for managing machine identities at scale. Large enterprises cannot rely on manual processes to provision, rotate, and revoke machine identities, as doing so introduces human error and operational inefficiencies. Automated identity orchestration platforms integrate with cloud providers, IAM solutions, and certificate authorities to enforce identity policies in real time. Just-in-time (JIT) credential provisioning ensures that machine identities are issued temporarily, expiring automatically when they are no longer needed. Automated key and certificate rotation prevents credential misuse by periodically refreshing encryption keys and authentication tokens without manual intervention.

Enterprises operating in multi-cloud and hybrid environments must establish consistent identity management frameworks across all platforms. Cloud providers offer native IAM services, but managing machine identities across AWS, Azure, Google Cloud, and on-premises infrastructure requires a unified approach. Federated identity management enables organizations to extend security policies across different cloud environments, ensuring that machine identities authenticate consistently regardless of their hosting provider. Identity federation also facilitates secure authentication between business partners, third-party vendors, and SaaS applications, reducing the need for separate credential management processes.

Monitoring and anomaly detection play a critical role in securing machine identities at scale. Security teams must continuously monitor machine identity activity to detect unauthorized access attempts, privilege escalations, and credential misuse. SIEM (Security Information and Event Management) platforms aggregate machine identity logs, providing real-time insights into authentication events and potential threats. AI-driven behavioral analytics enhance detection capabilities by identifying deviations from normal machine identity behavior, such as unexpected access patterns or excessive API calls. By integrating automated monitoring tools, enterprises can respond to identity-related security incidents proactively.

Compliance with regulatory requirements is a key consideration for large enterprises managing machine identities. Industry regulations such as GDPR, HIPAA, PCI-DSS, NIST, and ISO 27001 mandate strict identity governance policies, including encryption, access controls, and audit logging. Automated compliance enforcement helps organizations meet regulatory obligations by ensuring that machine identities adhere to security policies. Continuous compliance monitoring provides real-time audit trails that document identity usage, helping enterprises demonstrate compliance to auditors and regulatory bodies.

To further enhance security, large enterprises should adopt zero trust security models for machine identities. Traditional perimeter-based security models assume that authenticated identities should be inherently trusted. However, zero trust eliminates this assumption by requiring continuous identity verification at every access request. Machine identities must be authenticated dynamically based on risk assessments, security posture, and contextual factors such as device location and behavioral history. Implementing zero trust authentication reduces the risk of compromised machine identities being used for unauthorized access.

Securing DevOps environments is another critical aspect of machine identity management in large enterprises. DevOps teams frequently generate and use machine identities to automate infrastructure provisioning, CI/CD pipelines, and microservices communication. Without proper governance, secrets embedded in code repositories, configuration files, and container images can be inadvertently exposed. Integrating secrets management solutions within DevOps workflows ensures that API keys, SSH credentials, and digital certificates are stored securely, rotated regularly, and retrieved dynamically at runtime. Security controls should be embedded into CI/CD pipelines to enforce identity policies without disrupting development velocity.

Incident response planning must account for machine identity security incidents. Large enterprises should establish predefined workflows for detecting, investigating, and mitigating machine identity breaches. When a machine identity is compromised, security teams must have automated processes in place to revoke credentials, isolate affected workloads, and restore secure access. Integrating identity threat intelligence into incident response frameworks enables organizations to correlate identity-related attack patterns, assess risk levels, and prioritize remediation efforts. Regular security drills and penetration testing exercises help validate incident response readiness and identify areas for improvement.

The use of blockchain and decentralized identity frameworks is an emerging best practice for securing machine identities in large enterprises. Traditional identity management models rely on centralized authorities, which can become single points of failure. Decentralized identity models leverage blockchain technology to distribute identity verification across multiple nodes, reducing the risk of identity spoofing and unauthorized access. Organizations exploring decentralized identity solutions should evaluate the benefits of self-sovereign identities (SSIs) and cryptographic attestation mechanisms for machine identity authentication.

Ensuring that machine identity security aligns with business continuity planning is another important best practice. Machine identities are integral to enterprise operations, enabling automated workflows, cloud integrations, and encrypted communications. Any disruption to identity management services—such as certificate expirations, revoked API keys, or misconfigured IAM policies—can lead to service outages and operational downtime. Enterprises must establish failover mechanisms, redundant authentication pathways, and backup identity stores to ensure continuous availability of machine identities.

Cybersecurity awareness training should also extend to machine identity management. Many security teams focus on human identity governance but overlook the security risks associated with machine identities. Educating IT administrators, DevOps engineers, and security analysts on best practices for managing machine identities helps prevent misconfigurations, credential leaks, and privilege escalations. Organizations should incorporate machine identity security into broader cybersecurity awareness programs, reinforcing the importance of strong authentication and access control measures.

Large enterprises must continuously evolve their machine identity management strategies to address emerging threats, technological advancements, and regulatory changes. Conducting regular security assessments, refining access control policies, and adopting identity governance automation ensures that machine identities remain secure at scale. By implementing a holistic approach that integrates visibility, automation, monitoring, compliance, and zero trust principles, large enterprises can effectively manage the growing complexity of machine identities while reducing security risks and operational disruptions.

Overcoming Common Pitfalls in Machine Identity Management

Managing machine identities effectively is critical to securing enterprise systems, but many organizations encounter pitfalls that lead to security vulnerabilities, operational inefficiencies, and compliance risks. As the number of machine identities grows due to cloud adoption, automation, and interconnected systems, organizations must address these challenges proactively. Common pitfalls in machine identity management include lack of visibility, overprivileged credentials, poor lifecycle management, inadequate monitoring, and failure to integrate identity governance into security frameworks. Understanding these issues and implementing best practices helps organizations secure their machine identities while maintaining efficiency and compliance.

One of the most common pitfalls in machine identity management is the lack of visibility into machine identities across the enterprise. Many organizations do not have an accurate inventory of all API keys, service accounts, SSH keys, digital certificates, and cryptographic credentials used within their environments. Without visibility, security teams cannot track which identities are in use, where they are stored, or who has access to them. This lack of oversight leads to identity sprawl, where machine identities accumulate over time without proper management. Organizations must deploy automated discovery tools that continuously scan networks, cloud environments, and application repositories to identify all machine identities and ensure they are properly cataloged.

Another significant challenge is the improper assignment of privileges to machine identities. Many machine identities are created with excessive permissions, granting them access to more resources than necessary. Overprivileged service accounts, API tokens, and IAM roles increase the attack surface and can be exploited by attackers if compromised. Organizations must enforce the principle of least privilege, ensuring that machine identities receive only the minimum access required for their functions. Implementing role-based access control (RBAC) and attribute-based access control (ABAC) frameworks helps define granular permission policies that restrict access while maintaining operational flexibility.

Poor lifecycle management is another major pitfall in machine identity security. Many enterprises fail to implement structured processes for provisioning, rotating, and decommissioning machine identities. API keys, digital certificates, and cryptographic credentials often remain in use long after they are needed, creating security risks if they are compromised or misused. Expired or misconfigured certificates can cause authentication failures, leading to service disruptions. Organizations must automate lifecycle management by integrating identity governance platforms that enforce scheduled certificate renewals, key rotations, and automated deprovisioning of unused machine identities.

A lack of real-time monitoring and anomaly detection leaves organizations vulnerable to identity-based attacks. Machine identities are frequently targeted by cybercriminals seeking to exploit authentication mechanisms, escalate privileges, or exfiltrate data. Without continuous monitoring, organizations may fail to detect unauthorized access attempts, excessive authentication failures, or abnormal service-to-service communications. Security information and event management (SIEM) solutions, combined with machine learning-driven behavioral analytics, help detect suspicious machine identity activity in real time. Logging all identity-related authentication events and integrating alerts with security operations centers (SOCs) ensures rapid response to potential threats.

Another common mistake is failing to integrate machine identity management with broader cybersecurity frameworks. Many enterprises manage machine identities separately from human identities, leading to inconsistencies in access control policies and security enforcement. Machine identities should be governed under the same identity and access management (IAM) frameworks used for human authentication. Integrating machine identity security with IAM solutions, zero trust architectures, and security orchestration platforms ensures a unified approach to identity governance. Organizations must also extend multi-factor authentication (MFA) and continuous identity verification to machine identities where applicable, reducing the risk of credential compromise.

Hardcoded credentials in code repositories, configuration files, and scripts present another security weakness in machine identity management. Developers often embed API keys and service credentials directly into application code for convenience, but if these credentials are exposed in public repositories or internal repositories with weak access controls, attackers can exploit them. Organizations must implement secrets management solutions that store, encrypt, and dynamically inject credentials at runtime, eliminating the need for hardcoded secrets. Automated scanning tools should be deployed to detect and alert on exposed credentials in code repositories, preventing accidental leaks.

Misconfigured cloud identity permissions pose a major risk to machine identity security. Many cloud-based applications rely on IAM roles, service accounts, and managed identities to authenticate workloads, but organizations often grant excessive privileges or fail to enforce strict access controls. Attackers can exploit misconfigured cloud IAM settings to gain unauthorized access to cloud resources, manipulate infrastructure, or extract sensitive data. Organizations must regularly audit cloud IAM policies, enforce conditional access controls, and apply just-in-time (JIT) identity provisioning to minimize identity exposure.

Failure to revoke compromised or unused machine identities promptly can lead to long-term security vulnerabilities. Many breaches occur because organizations fail to detect and revoke credentials that have been compromised, reused, or abandoned. When a machine identity is no longer needed, it must be deactivated immediately to prevent unauthorized use. Automated revocation mechanisms should be in place to disable API keys, invalidate digital certificates, and revoke access tokens when a security incident is detected. Integrating incident response workflows with identity security ensures that compromised credentials are quickly contained and rotated.

Regulatory non-compliance due to weak machine identity governance is another challenge that enterprises must address. Regulations such as GDPR, HIPAA, PCI-DSS, and NIST require organizations to enforce strict identity management practices, including encryption, authentication, and audit logging. Failing to implement proper machine identity controls can result in regulatory violations, financial penalties, and reputational damage. Organizations must align their identity management policies with compliance requirements, implementing automated compliance reporting tools that generate audit trails and ensure adherence to industry standards.

Machine identity sprawl becomes increasingly difficult to manage as organizations scale their cloud and hybrid environments. Many enterprises struggle with managing machine identities across multiple cloud platforms, SaaS applications, and on-premises infrastructure, leading to fragmented security policies. Federated identity management provides a unified approach to securing machine identities across multi-cloud environments, allowing organizations to enforce consistent access controls, authentication mechanisms, and policy enforcement across different providers. Cloud-native security frameworks should be integrated with existing identity governance solutions to streamline machine identity management.

Another common pitfall is the lack of awareness and training around machine identity security. Many IT administrators, DevOps teams, and security professionals focus primarily on human identity governance, neglecting the risks associated with machine identities. Organizations must provide targeted training programs that educate teams on best practices for managing API keys, securing digital certificates, enforcing least privilege, and detecting identity-based threats. Security awareness campaigns should emphasize the importance of identity hygiene, encouraging teams to follow secure development and deployment practices.

Continuous improvement in machine identity management is necessary to keep pace with evolving threats. Organizations must conduct regular security assessments, penetration testing, and red team exercises to identify weaknesses in identity governance. Reviewing identity access logs, refining privilege policies, and adopting new automation technologies help enterprises stay ahead of emerging identity-based attack vectors. Security teams should also collaborate with industry peers, participate in threat intelligence sharing, and adopt best practices from security frameworks such as NIST's cybersecurity guidelines for identity management.

By proactively addressing these common pitfalls, organizations can strengthen their machine identity security, prevent credential-based attacks, and maintain a robust identity governance framework. Implementing automation, enforcing least privilege, monitoring identity activity, and integrating security policies across cloud environments ensures that machine identities remain secure, compliant, and resistant to exploitation.

Vendor Solutions and Tools for Machine Identity Protection

As machine identities become a growing target for cyber threats, organizations must leverage vendor solutions and security tools to protect their digital certificates, API keys, cryptographic credentials, and service accounts. Machine identity protection involves managing the lifecycle of identities, enforcing access controls, detecting anomalies, and automating security policies to prevent unauthorized access and credential misuse. Various cybersecurity vendors provide specialized solutions to address these challenges, offering automated certificate management, secrets management, identity governance, and monitoring tools designed to safeguard machine identities across hybrid and multi-cloud environments.

One of the key components of machine identity protection is certificate lifecycle management. Digital certificates authenticate machines, enable encrypted communications, and prevent unauthorized entities from spoofing trusted systems. However, manually managing thousands of certificates across an enterprise can lead to security gaps, such as expired certificates, misconfigured encryption, and certificate misuse. Vendors such as Venafi, DigiCert, and AppViewX provide automated certificate lifecycle management solutions that issue, renew, and revoke certificates in real time. These tools integrate with certificate authorities (CAs) to enforce consistent certificate policies, monitor expiration timelines, and prevent outages caused by expired credentials.

Secrets management solutions play a critical role in protecting machine identities by securely storing, rotating, and managing API keys, encryption keys, and authentication tokens. Traditional methods of storing secrets in configuration files, scripts, or code repositories introduce significant security risks, as exposed secrets can be exploited by attackers. Secrets management tools such as HashiCorp Vault, AWS Secrets Manager, Azure Key Vault, and CyberArk Conjur provide encrypted storage for machine credentials, ensuring that secrets are dynamically retrieved and rotated without manual intervention. These solutions also enforce access control policies, restricting secrets access to authorized users and applications while generating audit logs for security monitoring.

Cloud identity and access management (IAM) solutions help organizations enforce machine identity security across cloud platforms. Cloud providers such as AWS, Microsoft Azure, and Google Cloud offer native IAM tools that control how machine identities interact with cloud services. AWS IAM provides role-based access controls for workloads, Azure Managed Identities automate authentication for cloud applications, and Google Cloud IAM enables policy-based identity governance. These solutions integrate with security policies to enforce least privilege access, preventing overprivileged machine identities from being exploited. Additionally, cloud IAM tools provide detailed logging and monitoring features that track identity access attempts and privilege escalations.

Machine identity monitoring and anomaly detection are essential for detecting unauthorized activity and credential abuse. SIEM (Security Information and Event Management) platforms such as Splunk, IBM QRadar, and Microsoft Sentinel aggregate machine identity logs and apply behavioral analytics to detect suspicious authentication events. These tools analyze machine-to-machine interactions, identifying anomalies such as excessive API requests, unauthorized certificate use, or privilege escalations. AI-driven security platforms such as Exabeam and Darktrace enhance anomaly detection by using machine learning models to identify deviations from normal identity behavior, triggering alerts when potential security incidents are detected.

Privileged access management (PAM) solutions enhance machine identity security by controlling privileged credentials and restricting administrative access. Vendors such as CyberArk, BeyondTrust, and Thycotic offer PAM platforms that manage privileged machine identities, enforcing strict authentication policies and session monitoring. PAM tools prevent unauthorized access to critical infrastructure by requiring additional verification before privileged machine identities can be used. These solutions also record session activity, providing forensic insights in the event of a security breach.

Identity governance and administration (IGA) solutions provide policy-based identity lifecycle management for machine identities. Vendors such as SailPoint, Saviynt, and One Identity offer identity governance platforms that enforce role-based access policies, automate identity provisioning, and conduct periodic access reviews. These tools ensure that machine identities are only granted necessary permissions and automatically revoke access when identities are no longer in use. IGA solutions integrate with cloud IAM services and security frameworks, enabling organizations to maintain centralized control over machine identity governance while ensuring compliance with industry regulations.

Zero trust security solutions help organizations apply continuous authentication and authorization policies to machine identities. Zero trust platforms such as Zscaler, Palo Alto Networks Prisma Access, and Google BeyondCorp enforce strict identity verification for all machine interactions, regardless of network location. These solutions require machine identities to authenticate dynamically before accessing enterprise resources, reducing the risk of credential compromise. By implementing zero trust principles, organizations can ensure that machine identities are continuously validated based on risk assessments and contextual factors such as device health and behavioral history.

Threat intelligence platforms provide additional protection for machine identities by correlating real-time threat data with identity-related activity. Vendors such as CrowdStrike, Recorded Future, and FireEye offer threat intelligence solutions that identify known attack patterns targeting machine identities. These tools analyze global threat data, detecting compromised certificates, leaked API keys, and identity misuse within dark web marketplaces. Organizations can integrate threat intelligence feeds with identity management platforms to proactively detect machine identity threats and revoke credentials before they are exploited.

Blockchain-based decentralized identity solutions are emerging as an alternative to traditional identity management models. Vendors such as Evernym, Sovrin, and Microsoft ION provide decentralized identity frameworks that enable machine identities to be independently verified without relying on centralized certificate authorities. These solutions use blockchain technology to create tamper-proof identity records, reducing the risk of certificate forgery and unauthorized identity issuance. While still in early adoption, decentralized identity solutions offer promising advancements in secure, transparent, and trustless machine identity verification.

Automated remediation and response tools help organizations react quickly to machine identity breaches. Security orchestration, automation, and response (SOAR) platforms such as Palo Alto Networks Cortex XSOAR, Splunk Phantom, and IBM Resilient enable automated incident response workflows that revoke compromised machine identities, rotate affected credentials, and isolate impacted systems. By integrating SOAR platforms with identity governance and SIEM tools, organizations can automate containment measures, reducing the dwell time of attackers who exploit machine identities.

Regulatory compliance solutions ensure that machine identity management aligns with security frameworks such as GDPR, HIPAA, PCI-DSS, and NIST. Vendors such as LogicGate, OneTrust, and RSA Archer provide compliance automation platforms that generate audit reports, track identity access policies, and enforce regulatory controls.

These solutions help organizations document machine identity security practices, ensuring that identity management processes meet legal and industry standards.

By leveraging a combination of certificate lifecycle management, secrets management, cloud IAM, monitoring, PAM, IGA, zero trust, threat intelligence, and compliance solutions, organizations can build a comprehensive machine identity protection strategy. Integrating these tools into a unified security framework enables enterprises to reduce identity-related risks, detect anomalies in real time, and automate identity governance at scale. As machine identity threats continue to evolve, adopting vendor solutions tailored for machine identity protection ensures that organizations remain resilient against identity-based cyber threats while maintaining operational efficiency and compliance.

The Future of Identity Security Beyond Machines

As digital ecosystems continue to evolve, identity security is expanding beyond traditional human and machine identities. The rise of artificial intelligence, decentralized identity models, quantum-resistant cryptography, and the merging of physical and digital worlds are reshaping how identities are authenticated, managed, and secured. Identity security is no longer limited to managing user credentials and machine certificates; it now extends to autonomous systems, self-sovereign identities, biological authentication methods, and trust frameworks that transcend organizational and geopolitical boundaries. The future of identity security will require adaptive technologies, continuous authentication mechanisms, and new models of trust that can operate in an increasingly decentralized and automated world.

One of the most significant shifts in identity security is the increasing role of artificial intelligence and machine learning in both identity protection and cyber threats. AI-driven security platforms are being used to detect anomalies in authentication patterns, automatically adjust identity permissions based on real-time risk analysis, and provide continuous identity verification without human intervention. Behavioral biometrics, which analyze typing patterns, mouse movements, and voice recognition, are being integrated into identity security frameworks to provide an additional layer of continuous authentication. However, AI is also being weaponized by cybercriminals to generate deepfake identities, bypass authentication controls, and automate large-scale identity theft operations. The future of identity security must include AI-driven defense mechanisms that can counteract these evolving threats while maintaining user and machine authentication integrity.

Decentralized identity models are emerging as a revolutionary approach to digital identity security. Traditional identity management relies on centralized entities, such as governments, corporations, or cloud providers, to issue and verify identities. However, this approach introduces risks related to single points of failure, data breaches, and unauthorized tracking. Decentralized identity solutions, powered by blockchain and distributed ledger technology, offer a way for individuals and machines to control their own identities without relying on a central authority. Self-sovereign identities (SSI) allow users to own and manage their credentials, sharing only necessary information with verifiers without exposing their entire identity. This shift from centralized to decentralized identity management reduces fraud risks, enhances privacy, and eliminates reliance on third-party identity providers.

Quantum computing is another factor that will reshape identity security in the coming years. Current cryptographic methods, including RSA and ECC, are vulnerable to quantum attacks that could break encryption in minutes. This creates an urgent need for quantum-resistant cryptographic algorithms that can withstand future decryption capabilities. Organizations are beginning to explore post-quantum cryptography (PQC) solutions that will secure digital identities, machine authentication, and encrypted communications in a post-quantum world. The transition to quantum-safe identity security requires enterprises to audit their cryptographic infrastructure, replace vulnerable algorithms, and implement hybrid encryption models that ensure compatibility with both classical and quantum-resistant cryptographic methods.

Biometric authentication is playing an increasingly central role in identity security, extending beyond traditional fingerprint and facial recognition. Future identity frameworks will integrate multi-modal biometrics, combining physiological characteristics such as iris scans, heartbeat rhythms, and even brainwave signatures to authenticate individuals. Advancements in DNA-based authentication and subdermal microchip implants are being explored as new methods of identity verification. While these technologies offer stronger authentication security, they also introduce ethical and privacy concerns. The collection and storage of biometric data must be handled with extreme caution, ensuring compliance with data protection regulations and safeguarding against biometric identity theft.

The convergence of digital and physical identity security is another critical aspect of the future of identity management. The rapid adoption of smart cities, connected vehicles, and augmented reality environments necessitates identity authentication that seamlessly integrates across both digital and physical spaces. Digital passports, blockchain-based driver's licenses, and real-time location-based identity verification are becoming essential for secure interactions in interconnected urban infrastructures. As identity verification moves beyond static credentials, dynamic and adaptive authentication models will play a crucial role in securing access to both physical and digital environments.

The proliferation of identity-based attacks is also driving the need for continuous authentication models. Traditional authentication methods, such as usernames and passwords, rely on one-time verification at login, which is no longer sufficient in high-risk digital environments. Continuous authentication continuously evaluates identity risk throughout an entire session, adapting access permissions based on real-time security assessments. Factors such as device telemetry, geolocation tracking, behavioral biometrics, and environmental context contribute to a dynamic authentication model that reduces identity fraud while enhancing user experience.

The Internet of Things (IoT) and autonomous systems further complicate the future of identity security. Billions of connected devices, from smart appliances to industrial robots, require authentication mechanisms that can scale securely without human intervention. Identity frameworks for IoT devices must support low-latency authentication, automated certificate management, and trust models that prevent unauthorized device access. The use of cryptographic attestation and zero-trust principles will be essential in securing the machine-to-machine authentication landscape, ensuring that only trusted devices can communicate with critical enterprise systems.

Regulatory frameworks will continue to evolve to address emerging identity security challenges. Governments and industry regulators are implementing stricter identity protection laws to safeguard against identity fraud, unauthorized tracking, and misuse of biometric data. Global initiatives, such as the European Union's Digital Identity Wallet and the World Economic Forum's Global Digital Identity initiative, aim to establish standardized identity security practices across international borders. As regulatory requirements become more complex, organizations must adopt automated compliance tools that ensure adherence to identity governance laws while maintaining security best practices.

The future of identity security will also be shaped by advances in privacy-preserving technologies. Zero-knowledge proofs (ZKPs), which allow one party to prove knowledge of a piece of information without revealing the information itself, are being explored as a way to verify identities without exposing sensitive credentials. Homomorphic encryption, which enables computations on encrypted data without decrypting it, may allow secure identity verification without compromising privacy. These advancements are essential in creating identity systems that balance security, privacy, and usability in an era of increased digital surveillance and data exploitation.

The role of identity security is expanding beyond human and machine authentication into a broader digital trust framework that encompasses AI-driven entities, decentralized identities, quantum-resilient authentication, and integrated physical-digital security models. Organizations must prepare for these shifts by adopting forward-thinking identity strategies, investing in emerging authentication technologies, and ensuring that their identity management practices remain adaptable to future security challenges.

As identity security continues to evolve, the ability to establish, verify, and protect digital identities will become a fundamental requirement for participating in the digital economy, securing enterprise systems, and maintaining trust in an increasingly interconnected world.

Final Thoughts: The Evolving Security Landscape

The security landscape is in a constant state of evolution, driven by advancements in technology, shifting threat dynamics, and the increasing interconnectedness of digital ecosystems. Organizations must continuously adapt to emerging risks, ensuring that their security frameworks remain resilient against sophisticated attacks targeting human and machine identities. The role of identity security has expanded beyond traditional authentication mechanisms, now encompassing cryptographic protections, zero trust architectures, decentralized identity models, and AI-driven threat intelligence. As digital transformation accelerates, the importance of securing identities—both human and machine—has never been greater.

The rise of cloud computing, automation, and artificial intelligence has reshaped enterprise security strategies. While these technologies enable greater efficiency, scalability, and innovation, they also introduce new vulnerabilities that attackers can exploit. Machine identities, API keys, and service accounts have become prime targets for cybercriminals, who seek to bypass security controls and gain unauthorized access to sensitive data. Identity-based attacks, such as credential stuffing, phishing, and API abuse, have evolved in complexity, requiring organizations to adopt more advanced security measures. The shift towards a perimeterless security model necessitates stronger identity governance, continuous authentication, and real-time risk assessments to protect digital assets effectively.

Zero trust security has emerged as a fundamental principle in modern cybersecurity strategies. Traditional security models relied on implicit trust, where authenticated users or machines were granted broad access within an organization's network. However, this approach has proven inadequate in the face of sophisticated cyber threats. Zero trust frameworks enforce continuous verification, requiring all identities—whether human, machine, or workload—to authenticate at every access request. Implementing zero trust principles ensures that organizations minimize the risk of credential misuse, insider threats, and lateral movement attacks. Identity security now plays a central role in zero trust implementations, reinforcing the need for robust authentication, strict privilege controls, and dynamic access policies.

The expansion of artificial intelligence and machine learning has introduced both security opportunities and new risks. AI-powered security solutions enhance threat detection by analyzing vast amounts of authentication data, identifying anomalies, and predicting potential attacks. Automated security responses, driven by AI-driven analytics, allow organizations to mitigate threats in real time, reducing the window of opportunity for attackers. However, AI is also being weaponized by adversaries who use it to automate cyberattacks, create deepfake identities, and bypass traditional security controls. Organizations must integrate AI into their security frameworks while remaining vigilant against AI-driven threats that could compromise identity security.

The growing reliance on decentralized identity models represents another shift in the security landscape. Traditional identity management frameworks rely on centralized authorities, such as governments, enterprises, and certificate authorities, to issue and verify credentials. However, these centralized systems are vulnerable to breaches, data manipulation, and unauthorized surveillance. Decentralized identity solutions, built on blockchain and distributed ledger technology, offer a more resilient alternative, allowing users and machines to control their own identities without relying on a single entity. Self-sovereign identities (SSI) enable secure, verifiable credentials that reduce the risk of identity theft and unauthorized access. The adoption of decentralized identity models will reshape how trust is established in digital interactions, providing greater security and privacy for both individuals and organizations.

As quantum computing progresses, organizations must prepare for the impending impact on cryptographic security. Current encryption standards, such as RSA and ECC, are vulnerable to quantum attacks that could render traditional authentication mechanisms obsolete. Post-quantum cryptographic algorithms are being developed to ensure that identity security remains resilient in a post-quantum world. Organizations must proactively assess their cryptographic infrastructure, identify potential vulnerabilities, and transition to quantum-safe encryption methods. The shift to quantum-resistant identity security will require industry-wide collaboration, government regulation, and technological advancements to safeguard sensitive data and authentication mechanisms.

The increasing prevalence of biometric authentication is transforming identity security, offering stronger protection against identity fraud and credential theft. Biometric identifiers, such as fingerprint recognition, facial authentication, and iris scanning, provide a more secure and user-friendly authentication method than traditional passwords. However, the collection and storage of biometric data introduce new privacy concerns, as compromised biometric information cannot be easily changed or revoked. Organizations must implement strict data protection measures to ensure that biometric credentials are securely encrypted, anonymized, and stored in compliance with regulatory standards. The future of biometric security will likely involve multi-modal authentication, combining multiple biometric factors to enhance security while preserving user privacy.

Regulatory frameworks are evolving to address emerging security challenges and ensure compliance with identity protection standards. Governments and regulatory bodies are implementing stricter guidelines to prevent identity fraud, enforce data protection, and establish secure authentication practices. Regulations such as GDPR, CCPA, HIPAA, PCI-DSS, and NIST require organizations to enforce robust identity security policies, maintain audit logs, and protect sensitive credentials from unauthorized access. As regulatory requirements continue to expand, organizations must adopt automated compliance solutions that enable continuous monitoring, reporting, and policy enforcement. Ensuring compliance with global security regulations is essential for maintaining trust, avoiding legal repercussions, and protecting digital assets from cyber threats.

The convergence of digital and physical security further complicates identity management in modern enterprises. As smart cities, IoT ecosystems, and connected devices become more integrated into daily operations, identity security must extend beyond traditional IT environments. Digital passports, blockchain-based identity verification, and AI-driven access controls are becoming essential for securing physical spaces, ensuring that only authenticated identities can access critical infrastructure. Organizations must develop identity frameworks that bridge the gap between digital and physical security, enabling seamless authentication across multiple environments while mitigating the risk of unauthorized access.

The future of identity security will also require organizations to embrace continuous authentication models that go beyond static login credentials. Traditional username-password authentication is no longer sufficient to protect against identity theft, phishing attacks, and credential-based breaches. Continuous authentication evaluates identity risk throughout an entire session, using behavioral analytics, geolocation tracking, and contextual signals to verify authenticity dynamically. By implementing continuous authentication frameworks, organizations can detect unauthorized access attempts in real time, revoke compromised credentials instantly, and prevent attackers from maintaining persistence within enterprise networks.

Cybersecurity awareness and workforce training will remain critical components of identity security strategies. Many security breaches result from human errors, such as weak password management, phishing attacks, or misconfigured access controls. Organizations must invest in ongoing security education programs that train employees on identity protection best practices, secure authentication methods, and threat detection techniques. Security awareness initiatives should also extend to machine identity management, ensuring that IT administrators, developers, and DevOps teams follow secure coding, secrets management, and privilege enforcement practices.

As the security landscape continues to evolve, organizations must adopt a proactive, adaptive approach to identity security. The integration of AI-driven threat intelligence, zero trust architectures, quantum-resistant cryptography, and decentralized identity frameworks will be essential for mitigating future identity-based threats. Security teams must remain vigilant, continuously refining identity governance policies, monitoring authentication activity, and leveraging automation to enhance protection against credential misuse and unauthorized access.

Identity security is at the core of modern cybersecurity strategies, protecting not only individual users but also the vast networks of machines, applications, and automated systems that power today's digital economy. Organizations that prioritize identity security, invest in cutting-edge authentication technologies, and implement continuous monitoring frameworks will be better equipped to navigate the challenges of an evolving security landscape. The future of identity security requires resilience, innovation, and collaboration, ensuring that trust remains the foundation of digital interactions in an increasingly interconnected world.

Conclusion: Building a Resilient Machine Identity Strategy

Machine identity management has become an essential component of modern cybersecurity strategies as enterprises increasingly rely on digital certificates, cryptographic keys, service accounts, and API tokens to authenticate non-human entities. The rapid expansion of cloud computing, automation, and artificial intelligence has driven an exponential increase in the number of machine identities, creating new security challenges that organizations must address. Without a resilient machine identity strategy, enterprises face heightened risks of credential theft, unauthorized access, and identity-based attacks that could compromise critical business operations. Establishing a comprehensive and adaptable approach to machine identity management is essential for securing digital ecosystems while maintaining operational efficiency and compliance.

A resilient machine identity strategy begins with achieving full visibility into all machine identities within an organization. Many enterprises struggle with identity sprawl, where thousands of certificates, keys, and service accounts accumulate without proper oversight. Without clear visibility, security teams cannot effectively monitor or protect machine identities, leaving them vulnerable to exploitation. Implementing automated discovery tools that continuously scan networks, cloud environments, and application infrastructures helps organizations map out their identity landscape. A centralized inventory of machine identities enables security teams to track ownership, usage, and expiration dates, reducing the risk of unmanaged credentials being compromised.

Once visibility is established, organizations must enforce strict identity governance policies to manage the lifecycle of machine identities effectively. Identity governance ensures that credentials are issued, rotated, and revoked according to predefined security policies. Machine identities should not be granted excessive privileges or long-lived access, as doing so increases the likelihood of credential misuse. Automated lifecycle management solutions integrate with identity governance frameworks to enforce policies dynamically, ensuring that API keys, certificates, and cryptographic credentials are regularly updated and decommissioned when no longer needed. A policy-driven approach minimizes security gaps while enhancing operational efficiency.

The principle of least privilege is a foundational element of a resilient machine identity strategy. Overprivileged machine identities pose a significant risk, as attackers who compromise them can escalate privileges and gain unauthorized access to sensitive systems. Organizations must implement least privilege access controls by defining role-based and attribute-based policies that restrict machine identities to only the permissions necessary for their functions. Conducting periodic privilege audits helps security teams identify and remediate overprivileged identities, reducing the attack surface and mitigating the risk of unauthorized access. Least privilege enforcement is a proactive security measure that strengthens identity security while ensuring that machine identities operate within controlled parameters.

Automation plays a crucial role in scaling machine identity security. Managing machine identities manually in large enterprises is impractical and prone to human error. Automated solutions streamline identity provisioning, rotation, and revocation, eliminating the need for manual intervention. Just-in-time (JIT) identity issuance enhances security by granting temporary access credentials that expire once their purpose is fulfilled. Automated key rotation prevents credentials from becoming stagnant, reducing the risk of attackers exploiting long-lived access tokens. Integrating identity automation with security orchestration and response platforms enables enterprises to enforce identity policies consistently while maintaining agility in security operations.

Continuous monitoring and real-time anomaly detection are essential for identifying and mitigating machine identity threats. Attackers often target machine identities to conduct unauthorized API calls, deploy malware, or impersonate trusted systems. Security teams must implement real-time monitoring tools that track authentication attempts, privilege escalations, and unusual access patterns. SIEM (Security Information and Event Management) solutions aggregate identity-related logs, providing visibility into potential security incidents. AI-driven behavioral analytics further enhance detection capabilities by identifying deviations from normal machine identity behavior, allowing organizations to detect and respond to threats before they escalate.

Compliance and regulatory adherence are critical components of a resilient machine identity strategy. Industry regulations, including GDPR, HIPAA, PCI-DSS, and NIST, mandate strict identity governance policies to protect sensitive data and enforce access controls. Organizations must ensure that their identity management frameworks align with these regulatory standards by implementing encryption, authentication, and audit logging mechanisms. Automated compliance reporting tools simplify the process of generating audit logs and demonstrating regulatory adherence. Maintaining compliance not only protects enterprises from legal penalties but also strengthens overall security by enforcing standardized identity management practices.

The adoption of zero trust security models further reinforces machine identity resilience. Zero trust frameworks eliminate implicit trust, requiring continuous verification of all identities—whether human or machine—before granting access. Implementing zero trust authentication ensures that machine identities are validated dynamically based on risk assessments and contextual factors, such as device health, geolocation, and behavioral patterns. By integrating machine identity management with zero trust architectures, organizations can prevent unauthorized access, detect compromised credentials, and enforce security policies in real time.

Securing DevOps and cloud-native environments is another critical aspect of machine identity resilience. DevOps teams frequently generate and use machine identities for CI/CD pipelines, containerized applications, and automated infrastructure provisioning. Without proper governance, secrets stored in code repositories, configuration files, and container images can be inadvertently exposed. Organizations must integrate secrets management solutions into DevOps workflows to store, encrypt, and dynamically inject credentials at runtime. Enforcing security controls within CI/CD pipelines prevents credential leaks and ensures that machine identities are securely managed throughout the software development lifecycle.

Incident response planning must also incorporate machine identity security. When a machine identity is compromised, security teams must have predefined workflows to detect, contain, and remediate the breach. Automated response mechanisms enable rapid credential revocation, key rotation, and identity isolation, minimizing the impact of identity-based threats. Integrating machine identity security into incident response frameworks ensures that organizations can respond swiftly to breaches while maintaining business continuity. Regular security drills and tabletop exercises help security teams refine incident response procedures and identify potential areas for improvement.

As the digital landscape continues to evolve, organizations must remain adaptable in their approach to machine identity security. Emerging technologies, including quantum computing, AI-driven authentication, and decentralized identity models, will reshape the future of identity security. Preparing for these advancements requires a proactive mindset, continuous innovation, and collaboration between security teams, technology vendors, and regulatory bodies. Organizations that embrace adaptive security strategies will be better equipped to navigate the complexities of identity management while mitigating risks associated with evolving cyber threats.

A resilient machine identity strategy is not a one-time implementation but an ongoing process that requires continuous evaluation, refinement, and adaptation. Organizations must invest in identity security automation, enforce strict access controls, integrate real-time monitoring, and align their strategies with regulatory frameworks. By prioritizing identity governance, implementing proactive security measures, and leveraging advanced identity protection technologies, enterprises can build a strong foundation for securing machine identities in an increasingly interconnected digital world. A well-executed machine identity strategy not only enhances cybersecurity resilience but also ensures the integrity, confidentiality, and trustworthiness of digital interactions across enterprise ecosystems.